LEGION CONDOR

Legion Condor

History • Organization • Aircraft • Uniforms • Awards • Memorabilia
1936-1939

Raúl Arias, Lucas Molina, and Rafael Permuy

4880 Lower Valley Road • Atglen, PA 19310

Dedication by Jose Manuel Campesino Bilbao:

To my wife Mª Victoria whose dedication and generosity I have always admired.

Copyright © 2013 by Schiffer Publishing, Ltd.
Library of Congress Control Number: 2013937224

All rights reserved. No part of this work may be reproduced or used in any form or by any means—graphic, electronic, or mechanical, including photocopying or information storage and retrieval systems—without written permission from the publisher.

The scanning, uploading and distribution of this book or any part thereof via the Internet or via any other means without the permission of the publisher is illegal and punishable by law. Please purchase only authorized editions and do not participate in or encourage the electronic piracy of copyrighted materials.

"Schiffer," "Schiffer Publishing Ltd. & Design," and the "Design of pen and inkwell" are registered trademarks of Schiffer Publishing Ltd.

Printed in China.
ISBN: 978-0-7643-4341-4

This book was originally published under the title,
Legión Cóndor: Estructura de una Fuerza de Combate, by Galland Books, Spain.

We are interested in hearing from authors with book ideas on related topics.

Published by Schiffer Publishing Ltd.
4880 Lower Valley Road
Atglen, PA 19310
Phone: (610) 593-1777
FAX: (610) 593-2002
E-mail: Info@schifferbooks.com.
Visit our web site at: www.schifferbooks.com
Please write for a free catalog.
This book may be purchased
from the publisher.
Try your bookstore first.

Contents

Introduction
The Luftwaffe: The Origins of Hitler's Air Force   7

Chapter I
Notes on the German Intervention   29

Chapter II
The Role Played by the Air Force   93

Chapter III
The Role Played by Ground Forces: Imker-Gruppe   205

Chapter IV
The Role Played by the Navy   233

Chapter V
Miscellaneous   243

Bibliography   291

Introduction

THE LUFTWAFFE:
THE ORIGINS OF HITLER'S AIR FORCE

Por Carlos Caballero Jurado

When Hitler decided to support the Spanish *Alzamiento* (Uprising) of July 18, 1936 against the left-wing government of the *Frente Popular* and chose this as the instrument to provide that support, the German air force was a little over one year old Luftwaffe, since until March 1935 it had not officially existed. This fact may not be as well-appreciated as it should be when analyzing the role played by the Legion Condor in the Spanish Civil War.

Germany had been one of the pioneer countries in aviation and soon boasted a number of renowned designers and important aeronautical construction companies. As a result, during the First World War Germany had built up a powerful air force, divided between the army and the navy. When the war began, the Imperial German Army had a modest fleet of 218 aircraft and twelve Zeppelins, but during the war years German industry was able to manufacture over 40,000 military aircraft.

Loading ammunition
Any weapon or explosive was good for firing at or dropping on the enemy. These were the days of the First World War and the air arm was beginning to make its presence felt on the battlefields of Europe.

Fokker D-VII
One of the fighter planes used by the German during the First World War.

The victors of the war were well aware of how dangerous the German military air force could become and in the Treaty of Versailles which they imposed on Germany they took severe measures to avert the threat. The Germans were obliged to hand over or destroy all their military air fleet (with close to 20,000 aircraft in service in 1918) and, more importantly, to totally dismantle their aircraft manufacturing capacity. They were also prohibited from forming even the most modest air force within the scant military organization that was permitted in Germany, the Reichswehr. To avoid the danger of aircraft with military capabilities being built under the guise of civil aircraft, very precise limits were set regarding the characteristics of the aircraft which could be built in Germany, with stringent limits on range, speed, ceiling, load capacity, etc. It is no surprise that Anthony

Transport aircraft
Right. Junkers Ju 52 3m. It was developed by Junkers as a transport plane and a bomber, providing very good service for both the Luftwaffe and Lufthansa.

Fokker, the experienced Dutch designer who had created one of the most important German aeronautical companies in the First World War, famous for its fighters, left Germany and returned to his native Holland. Some companies had to move their production to other countries; one such example was Dornier, which manufactured aircraft in Holland, Japan and Switzerland. The legendary three-engined Junkers Ju 52 started out being built in the Soviet Union, where Junkers had a factory, and also in Sweden, and only later could it be produced in Germany.

Anthony Fokker
Dutch engineer whose fighter aircraft designs plied the skies of Europe in the First World War.

Introduction

***Jagdstaffel* "Richthofen"**
At center is commander Manfred von Richthofen, the famous "Red Baron." Many of his pilots would be the creators of the new Luftwaffe, men who started working towards that goal in the late-1920s.

The German aeronautical industry was practically reduced to a cottage industry, with tiny factories mainly producing light recreational aircraft. The fact that in 1922 the German aircraft industry manufactured a total of just forty-seven aircraft is testimony to the hard times that had befallen it. It was not until 1926 when the draconian restrictions were partly lifted within the framework of what is known as the "Paris Air Agreement." This breathed life into an industry that seemed to be on the brink of extinction.

The strict limitations on troop strength imposed on the Reichswehr and the prohibition of compulsory military service left little scope for trying to maintain at least some men with training as pilots, even if they had no aircraft to fly. However, with the forward thinking which characterized him, *General* Von Seeckt, the true brain behind the Reichswehr, succeeded in ensuring that a number of officers who had made names for themselves as pilots in the First World War could continue their military career in the Reichswehr; men like Helmuth Felmy, Hugo Sperrle and Manfred von Richtofen, to name but a few of the pilots we shall be talking about in this book. As all of them had training in the artillery, infantry, etc., it was possible to find them positions where they would remain active, and so prevent their training as airmen from being wasted. But the numbers tell their story; fewer than two hundred of all Reichswehr officers had served as pilots in the Great War.

What the Treaty of Versailles could not eradicate was the interest that the German people in general, and its engineers in particular, had in aviation. Which is why ultimately a certain number of aeronautical companies survived and some new ones sprung up. Ernst Heinkel, for example, who had been chief engineer at Albatros, took the bold step of starting up his own company in 1922. Years later it would become the favorite manufacturer of Spanish aircrews fighting on the Nationalist side.

Hugo Sperrle
He was an outstanding pilot in the First World War and continued his career in the Reichwehr. He would be the Legion Condor's first General.

Ernst Heinkel
German engineer and designer of a saga of aircraft that played a leading role in the Second World War.

Making a virtue of necessity, and given that the Treaty of Versailles imposed so many restrictions on conventional aircraft, the Germans developed an extraordinary passion for gliders, and 1925 saw the birth of the *Deutsche Forschungsinstitut für Segelflug* (German Glider Research Institute), whose acronym, DFS, would be popularized in the Second World War due to the gliders designed there. Thousands of future Luftwaffe pilots first took to the air in gliders and of course in World War II nobody used these devices to such great effect as the Germans. The numerous gliding clubs which were scattered all over Germany enjoyed the discreet patronage of the Reichswehr. A patronage which was not limited to gliders, but was extended to any civil flying club where the lucky owners of light aircraft, lovers of hot air ballooning, or even model aircraft fans pursued their hobbies.

The Reichswehr also took an interest in civil aviation. In 1926, two pre-existing companies merged to form Lufthansa, which very soon established a comprehensive network of routes across Europe, while becoming a leading company in trans-Atlantic flights to the Americas, especially South America. It quickly became one of the most important airlines in the world. It was headed by Erhard Milch, who had served in the First World War as a pilot and later, as we will see, became the true creator of the Luftwaffe. Lufthansa would be the instrument whereby many of the future officers of the Luftwaffe would be trained as pilots. Also its orders for aircraft served to keep the German aeronautical industry

Badge
The badge of the *Deutscher Luftsport Verband*, the German air sports association.

Model airplane hobby
Right. A Berlin boy of the *Hitlerjugend* checking the Kramo 10 engine of his model airplane.

INTRODUCTION

Gliders
Members of the Hitler Youth prepare a glider. Through its sporting associations the Nazi party encouraged flying in all types of gliders.

Erhard Milch
Below. From director of Lufthansa, Erhard Milch became the organizer of the new Luftwaffe, together with his friend and former comrade at arms, Hermann Göring. In the photo, with a cine camera, during the Second World War.

Within Germany itself, the task of creating any kind of "camouflaged" military air force unit or training military professionals to fly was more difficult. Observers of the Allied Control Council, which monitored compliance with the restrictive clauses imposed on Germany, were everywhere and would have spotted any such initiative immediately. Instead, the Reichswehr made use of secret military treaties entered into between the Weimar Republic and the Soviet Union in 1922. Thus the only military personnel who received combat flying training during this entire period did so at Lipetsk, in Russia, where the Germans shared an air base with the Soviets. Once again the number of men who received training as combat pilots there is revealing: just 120 men. Some models of military aircraft which the Reichswehr ordered from German manufacturers were evaluated at Lipetsk. They left the country disassembled and were assembled once they were in Russia. Among the aircraft evaluated at Lipetsk were two models which served in Spain; the Heinkel He 45 and the Heinkel He 46. The total number of these aircraft designed for military purposes and manufactured clandestinely between 1922 and 1933 was a meager 365 aircraft, a ridiculous figure (fewer than thirty-five aircraft a year), which put Germany behind countries with a far inferior demographic and technological potential, such as Poland and Czechoslovakia.

Heinkel He 45
One of the biplanes which Heinkel equipped the embryonic Luftwaffe with was the He 45. It was an observation aircraft and light bomber that would be used extensively in Spain after April 1937.

Of course there was no military aviation branch within the command structure of the Reichswehr. The few officers involved in the matter acted under the guise of small departments devoted to matters of "air defense." But German society was united in its desire to revise the Treaty of Versailles. Furthermore, with the passage of time, the hatred engendered by the war was cooling, and Germany was emerging from its condition as a "pariah State." Germany started to be readmitted into the international community and, as from 1926, it was allowed to be a member of the League of Nations. In military circles it was reckoned to be a matter of time before the victors of 1918 permitted Germany a certain degree of rearmament, so plans were made in that respect quite some time before Hitler came to power. In 1930, one of the aviation specialists of the Reichswehr High Command, the aforementioned Felmy – at that time *Oberstleutnant* – presented a plan to create a clandestine air force between 1931 and 1937, which could be activated in the event of war. The plan detailed the aircraft that should be produced, what units it would be necessary to create (twenty-two squadrons), and how they would be subordinated to land units. A bolder plan from the same officer, in February 1932, spoke of the need to have eighty squadrons by 1938, with a total of 720 aircraft, plus another 240 to be held in reserve. His plans met with a lukewarm response and in July 1932 the only measure the German military top brass dared to propose was the establishment of some air force training units in the period 1933-1934. Among the reasons behind the skepticism of the military high command was the disastrous economic situation into which Germany had slumped as a result of the economic crisis of 1929, which naturally affected the nation's coffers and also the weak aeronautical industry.

Helmuth Felmy
Having fought in the First World War as a German air force pilot, in 1930 he submitted a detailed plan to create a powerful clandestine air force.

INTRODUCTION

The "Red Baron"
Left. Manfred von Richthofen, famous World War I fighter ace, with the coveted medal for valor, *"Pour le Mérite"* (Blue Max), around his neck. After his death in combat he would be succeeded by a young pilot named Hermann Göring.

The situation changed radically when Hitler came into power on January 30, 1933. Not only because Hitler was determined to free Germany from the restrictions imposed at Versailles on German military power, which automatically implied rearming, but also, and more importantly, because his right-hand man was Hermann Göring. From the privileged political posts he would hold in the Third Reich he did everything in his power to maximize the potential of "his" Luftwaffe.

On February 2, a matter of hours after coming to power, Hitler appointed Göring to the office of Reich Commissioner for Aviation, which soon (in March) would become the all new Ministry of Aviation. This new governmental structure absorbed the aeronautical competencies that had previously been handled by the Ministry of Transport and the Ministry of the Interior, and it continued to be essentially a "civil" ministry. But not for long.

Despite the fact that in the Great War he had been decorated with the prestigious *"Pour le Mérite"* (or "Blue Max") medal and had taken over the command of the fighter wing previously led by the legendary "Red Baron," as a result of restrictions on personnel, Hermann Göring had left the army in 1920 with the rank of *Hauptmann*.

Göring
After commanding the legendary German Fighter Wing in the First World War, Hermann Göring left the army in 1920 with the rank of *Hauptmann*, and worked in Denmark and Sweden before entering politics.

Bruno Loerzer
Below. A former World War I fighter ace who led the *Deutscher Luftfahrt-Verband*. From the Ministry of Aviation he controlled its development as a school for future military airmen.

Like so many other German pilots, he chose to emigrate in order to work in the aeronautical industry of other countries (in his case, Denmark and Sweden), before returning to Germany to make a name for himself in politics as a high-ranking member of Hitler's NSDAP (National Socialist German Workers' Party). As an example of his importance, from August 1932 he was President of the *Reichstag*, the German parliament.

In August 1933 Göring received a meteoric promotion to the rank of *General der Infanterie* (equivalent to an American three-star general). The reason behind the promotion was because, as from that month, his ministry would be of an increasingly military nature. The Ministry of Defense (headed by *General* Werner von Blomberg) transferred its small and semi-clandestine air force general staff to the recently established Ministry of Aviation.

Already prior to that date the Ministry of Aviation had taken some very significant steps. In March 1933, what had up until then been a mere federation of recreational flying clubs, the *Deutscher Luftfahrt Verband* (German Aviation Association, DLV), became an organization directly under the control of the ministry, which appointed Bruno Loerzer. Loerzer had been a fighter ace in World War I and he would go on to hold important commands in World War II. All civil flying clubs were obliged to join

Introduction

General der Infanterie
Previous page, above. In the photo, taken in 1934, we see Göring, behind Hitler and Blomberg, in the uniform of Heer *General der Infanterie*. The Luftwaffe was still just a dream ... about to become a reality. BA.183-2008-1016-502.

Collection bucket
The sports associations of the NSDAP collected money to finance their activities. This bucket is collecting for sports aviation.

Badge
Right. A badge of the *Reichsluftschutzbund,* or National Air Defense League.

the new DLV, which also controlled the small flying components of the Nazi private armies, the SA and SS. As before, the range of activities undertaken by the DLV included everything from model airplanes, gliders, and ballooning to powered aircraft. It was organized along paramilitary lines and many consider it to be *de facto* the Luftwaffe at this time, albeit still with the thinnest of disguises. However, the DLV had no power of compulsory recruitment, although its uniformed members soon earned themselves a reputation for their propaganda and recruitment campaigns, aimed at engaging the public's interest in the world of flying.

During the period between the wars, civil associations concerned with disseminating self-defense measures against air raids sprang up all over Europe. Germany, of course, was no exception, since the country had suffered air raids against cities in the First World War and was now virtually defenseless against the threat. In April 1933 all existing civil passive defense associations were incorporated into the *Reichsluftschutzbund* (State Air Protection Corps, RLB) reporting directly to the Air Ministry. The first president of the RLB was Hugo Grimme, who had recently retired with the rank of *Brigadegeneral* and since the First World War had been an anti-aircraft

General Christiansen
Right. A veteran military pilot who headed the *NS-Fliegerkorps*. Like the rest of his colleagues he wore the Blue Max around his neck.

artillery specialist (in fact in 1935 he rejoined the Luftwaffe to serve in the *Flakartillerie*). Membership of this organization was voluntary, but just one year after its creation it boasted nearly two million members (Hitler set an example by joining). Inevitably, given the thinking that reigned in the Third Reich, it was a uniformed organization structured along paramilitary lines.

The most important changes were not as visible as has just been described. The challenge facing the Air Ministry was enormous. In March 1933, and to mention just the countries bordering on Germany, the French air force had over 3,000 aircraft, Poland had 700, Czechoslovakia 650, and Belgium 350. The first air rearmament plan passed by Göring in May 1933 aimed to provide fewer than 300 military aircraft in the course of one year. And the first squadrons formed in February 1933 with already existing aircraft were disguised as *Reklame-Staffel* (advertising squadrons), since their function in theory was to tow advertising banners through the skies of Germany.

In reality these three squadrons were formed with personnel from clandestine military sections of a number of German flying clubs and with pilots who had been trained at Lipetsk (incidentally, this clandestine German air base in Russia was summarily shut down by order from Hitler just after he came to power, due to his fervent anti-communism). The new Nazi authorities feared a swift and decisive military reaction from the victors of 1918 and from countries like Poland and Czechoslovakia, so they did everything possible to camouflage their first steps.

Airmen
Below. The training of military airmen was aided by the fact that many of them belonged to sport flying associations.

Introduction

Arado Ar 68 F
Above. One of the aircraft used in the early days of the Luftwaffe was this fighter, built by Arado Flugzeugwerke.

However, between early February 1933 and April 1935, the number of workers employed by the German aeronautical industry rose from 3,988 to 65,500; in other words, it increased by a factor of 16.4. Of the latter figure, most (43,800) worked in aircraft production plants, another significant number (19,200) was employed in aero engine factories, and the remainder worked in industries specializing in various accessories (such as radio equipment). This dizzying growth was due to the fact that the first and still half-hearted plan signed by Göring was replaced by other, far more audacious, plans implemented by the aforementioned Milch, who was Secretary of State in the Air Ministry and the man who was really "at the helm" (Göring's many political activities kept him too busy to play a more active role). The aeronautical industry soon became aware of the plans for air rearmament and, under the direction of the Ministry, expanded and improved their facilities. Bankrupt companies were refloated, others moved their activity from other countries back to the Reich. In the case of the vitally important company, Junkers, the State took over most of the shares and put in a new, dynamic management. Even more remarkable was that companies which until then had had nothing to do with aeronautics also turned their hand to it. Such was the case of Henschel, which had previously specialized in the manufacture of railway equipment, or Blohm & Voss, a shipbuilding concern.

Heinkel He 70
Below. Due to its speed it was nicknamed "Blitz," which in English is "Lightning." It was used by Lufthansa as a transport aircraft and would be used by the new Luftwaffe as a reconnaissance aircraft and bomber.

Breast eagle
Left. Like the Heer and the Kriegsmarine, the Luftwaffe had its own badge to be placed on the right breast of uniforms.

But what aircraft should they build? The question raises two issues. The first was whether to opt for existing models or ones that could be developed without too great an effort, or to develop more state-of-the-art models. As there was a need to create an air force as quickly as possible, a mixed solution was chosen. It was decided to build aircraft that were actually going to be obsolete almost from the outset, while more advanced models were designed and appraised which, in time, would provide a clear qualitative advantage. So we find that many of the aircraft produced in the mid-1930s did not form part of the Luftwaffe's fleet of aircraft at the start of the war. However, they did serve two important purposes; they provided training for the large number of workers who were entering the aeronautical industry for the first time, and who were largely unskilled in that industry, and they served to train pilots. The figures for 1934 give us an accurate idea of the situation in those early days. Of the nearly 2,000 aircraft that were built in the Reich, 65% were used for training pilots while the combat aircraft *per se* were all obsolete models. It is significant that Göring would try, albeit unsuccessfully as it turned out, to buy Italian Fiat CR-30 fighters which were better than anything the Germans were able to produce at that time.

Milch and Osterkamp
Previous page. Erhard Milch and Theo Osterkamp, two former comrades-in-arms of the First World War, were both leading players in the planning of the new Luftwaffe.
It is very interesting to note the design of the uniform worn by Milch, a uniform of the very earliest days of the Luftwaffe, which instead of the eagle on the breast had the badge of the *Deutscher Luftsport Verband*, while the cap bore the party eagle badge and an embryonic cockade, adorned with some small wings.
BA.183-2008-1016-507

Air Ministry
Right. Hermann Göring strove relentlessly to create an air force that would match those of the most important countries surrounding Germany.

Of even greater importance was the answer to the second question: what should Germany's air force be like? During the period between the wars a great deal of literature had appeared on the subject of the bombing of cities as the weapon which would decide wars in the future. Some of that literature was in the form of "futuristic novels" whose content was apocalyptic in tone. Of greater significance was the fact that several military theoreticians reached the conclusion that war waged with heavy bombers would in fact be the key to victory in future conflicts. In 1921, the Italian General Dohuet prophesied just that in his book *"The Command of the Air."* In 1923, in his book *"The Reformation of War,"* the famous and influential British Major-General J.F.C. Fuller, another keen advocate of the application of modern technologies to warfare (such as the tank) also made a conclusive diagnosis: the massive use of air forces against the enemy rearguard could achieve a swift and relatively bloodless victory. Even more explicit were the conclusions of another British author, J.M. Spaight, who in 1924 published a remarkable work: *"Air Power and War Rights."* He has been acclaimed as the most prolific 20th century British author on the subject of air power. The thesis of his work was clear: the bombing of enemy cities was permissible and could not be condemned under international law. In *"Air Power and the Cities"* (1930) he develops this thesis.

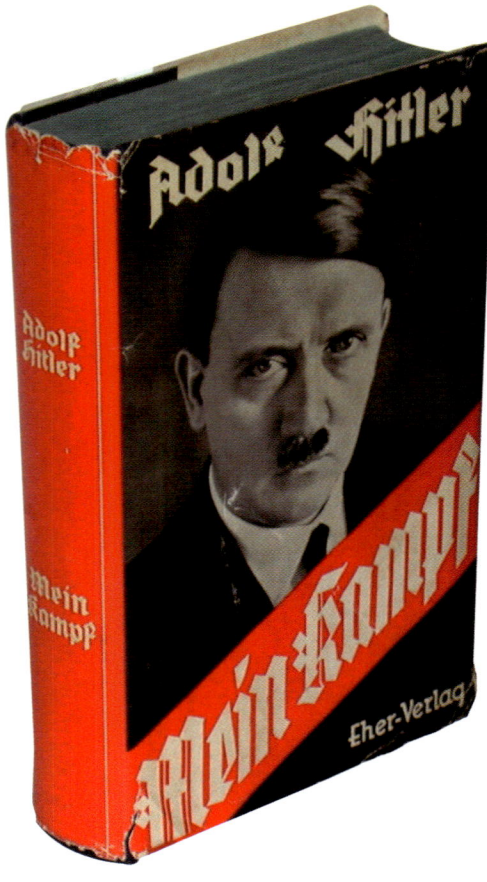

Mein Kampf
The book that Adolf Hitler wrote in Landsberg prison became a bestseller in Germany at the time.

Junkers Ju 86
One of the twin-engined bombers built in the mid-1930s.

Introduction

Stalin
Right. It was necessary to have a strategic air capability to attack the USSR beyond the Urals, where the Soviet dictator located his industrial capacity.

Inevitably these ideas aroused a certain amount of interest in Germany. In May 1933, a senior executive of Lufthansa, Robert Knauss, submitted a plan to Göring detailing what the future German Air Force should be like. Based on the writings of the aforementioned authors, Knauss's plan called for the rapid construction of a large fleet of four-engined bombers, capable of destroying the cities of countries like France and Poland if they attacked Germany. According to his calculations, that was the quickest way to provide Germany with a major deterrent capability. To build a large fleet of heavy bombers was faster and cheaper than building a handful of warships and much more decisive than forming a number of new infantry divisions.

Von Blomberg
German Minister of Defense in 1935. He gave Göring all the help he could to create the new air force.

An influential figure in the ministry, Walther Wever, chief of the clandestine General Staff that had been set up in that ministry to shape the future Luftwaffe, also adopted a similar position. Based on his reading of Hitler's *"Mein Kampf"*, which states that the German goal in foreign policy should be to conquer the USSR and expand territorially eastwards, Wever reached the conclusion that it was necessary to have an eminently strategic air force, so as to be able to attack remote regions, beyond the Urals, where Stalin had set up most of the USSR's industrial capacity under his five-year plans. Unlike Knauss (ultimately an amateur), Wever was a professional soldier (a magnificent general staff officer, albeit with no aeronautical experience, it has to be said) so his analysis was more nuanced. Although a major strategic component was necessary, the future Luftwaffe could not fail to address the need to support ground and sea forces, so a strong tactical component was also necessary. (Wever died in 1936, by which time he was Chief of General Staff of the Luftwaffe with the rank of *General*).

Students
A group of students observe the engine of this light biplane trainer, a Focke-Wulf Fw 44 Stieglitz.

Knauss's theories were soon forgotten while Wever's were developed towards giving more importance to the tactical component. In fact, from the outset, the future Luftwaffe embraced a clear commitment to becoming an arm that would provide ground forces with support. This is hardly surprising, since the vast majority of its officers were drawn from the army.

When the Air Ministry was set up, it would have been logical and natural for the Ministry of Defense to cry foul, and for them to have wanted to keep control over the future air force. In fact the opposite occurred. The minister, *General* Werner von Blomberg, could not have been more helpful. He told his subordinates that they should not hesitate to transfer their best officers to the air force which was being secretly organized, so that its corps of officers would be a true elite with a bold and courageous spirit. For January 1934 there were already nearly 300 commanders and officers, and some 1,600 NCOs and soldiers of the German army serving in the units that were secretly being set up by the Air Ministry. It was not until that year, 1934, when the clandestine air force began its own recruitment of men (under conditions of great secrecy, naturally), but even so, until 1935 when the Luftwaffe officially came into being, these men had to be trained in military academies belonging to the army or the navy.

Ernst Udet
Below. World War I fighter ace and the man responsible for the technical development of new aircraft for the Luftwaffe since 1935.

Introduction

Heinkel He 51
The Luftwaffe's standard fighter in 1936. Its shortcomings, when compared to its rivals, were revealed during the Spanish Civil War.

Junkers Ju 52
One of the best designs to come out of Junkers was this three-engined transport and bomber, which in various versions saw service with the Spanish Air Force right up until the 1970s.

The "terrestrial" origin of the new Luftwaffe goes a long way to explain its orientation towards cooperation with ground forces. But there are other reasons. To a great extent it was due to the influence of pilots like Ernst Udet, a World War I fighter ace, recipient of the *"Pour le Mérite,"* and who since June 1936 was responsible for the technical development of new aircraft for the Luftwaffe. As a great defender of dive-bomber and fighters, he rejected the idea of "strategic" bombing.

The truth of the matter was that the German military establishment was characterized by its high level of professionalism, and when the theories on the "decisive" effects of apocalyptic bombers were duly tested in appropriate exercises, it was discovered that the real effects were much less decisive than had been expected. However, when deployed in support of ground forces, the air force could be decisive on the battlefield. Given the choice between speculation (concerning the effectiveness of four-engined bombers) and experience (the effectiveness of light and medium bombers, some capable of dive-bombing raids, and of fighter and reconnaissance aircraft) the latter option was chosen. Because, furthermore, Germany could not afford the luxury of having a "dual" air force, one both tactical and strategic. There simply was not enough money.

Given the subject matter of this book, it is very important to compare the development of the aeronautical industry in the early years of Nazi rule and the same industry in the Soviet Union. Compared to the 1,968 military aircraft built in Germany in 1934, the USSR produced 3,109. As has already been mentioned, in the case of the Germans most of these were essentially trainers. But in that year, among the materiel received by the soviet air force were 570 fighters and 392 bombers, mostly of modern design, compared with the 109 fighters of an obsolete design (such as the Arado Ar 64 and Ar 65) and 240 transport aircraft hastily modified to serve as bombers (Dornier Do 11 and Junkers Ju 52) which were delivered in Germany. Aircraft such as the Dornier Do 17, Heinkel He 111, and Junkers Ju 86 medium bombers and the Ju 87 dive-bomber only existed on the drawing board. The former of those mentioned was actually the development of a aircraft originally designed as a passenger plane. All of them would fly in Spain. Although in general they were very advanced designs, it is also true that one of them (the Ju 86) would be a resounding failure.

In 1935 the gap between the total figures closed and Germany produced 3,183 military aircraft versus the 3,259 built by the USSR. But the qualitative difference persisted, since the USSR air force received 776 fighters and fifty-

Cockpit
Above. The Heinkel He 111 was the German bomber par excellence, both in the Spanish Civil War and World War II.

Bücker Bü 131
Light trainer biplane. This aircraft was given the name *"Jungmann"* (Young Man) and served as a basic trainer in the Luftwaffe and in other air forces, including the Spanish Air Force, until the late-1960s.

Introduction

nine bombers while the German force took delivery of 276 fighters and 165 bombers, albeit and once again obsolete models. It was not until 1936 when the Luftwaffe test center at Rechlin would begin to fly aircraft like the Messerschmitt Me 109 and Me 110, the Dornier Do 17, the Junkers Ju 87 and Ju 88 and the Henschel Hs 123.

On February 26, 1935, it was officially announced that Germany was reintroducing conscription. Months before, the "camouflage" measures aimed at concealing the budding air force had gradually been dismantled. And finally, on March 10, in an interview with the British daily newspaper, "The Daily Mail," Göring announced to the world the existence of the Luftwaffe. Meanwhile, several German leaders, including Hitler, announced over various media that the new air force now had a capability similar to that of the Royal Air Force. Of course it was not true, but it was hoped that the announcement would be enough to dissuade neighboring countries from attacking Germany.

The people that the Germans did not want to frighten were the British, with whom Hitler hoped to reach an agreement to share power. The British were the target of a great many friendly gestures, including invitations to visit German air bases to see all the different models and types of aircraft. Göring openly told these British envoys that his dream was that one day the British and Germans together would attack the Soviet Union to eradicate communism from the world.

This German propaganda attack could not be said to have had the desired effect. On the contrary, the British saw the birth of the Luftwaffe as a threat similar to the one posed before the Great War by the "Tirpitz Plan," whereby the Germans planned to have a large fleet of surface vessels. The British began to warn of the terrible danger of the Luftwaffe against which it would have to defend itself. They were quick to attribute to the Luftwaffe the type of plans which in fact only they were considering; *i.e.* the terror bombing of enemy cities. In this context of propaganda fueled tension we can better understand why the British press inflated events such as the bombing of Guernica.

Heinkel He 51
The fighter squadrons of Group J/88 were equipped with these antiquated aircraft until the arrival of the Messerschmitt Bf 109.

Junker Ju 160
The single-engine Ju 160 was designed to carry six passengers. The V-2 prototype was the military version.

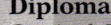

When all pretence was abandoned in the spring of 1935 and the Luftwaffe made its public appearance as the new third arm of the armed forces, its officer corps was formed by just 1,100 officers (900 in flying units and 200 in Flak anti-aircraft artillery units) while NCOs and soldiers numbered 17,000. By August 1939 the officer corps had grown to 15,000 with 370,000 men under their command. In other words, the number of officers had multiplied by fourteen and that of NCOs and soldiers by twenty-two, in a little over four years! This may be the highest growth rate ever experienced by an air force in peacetime.

We mentioned Flak, the anti-aircraft artillery, earlier as a branch of the Luftwaffe and, indeed, among its combat units, the German air force not only had flying units but also a large number of anti-aircraft artillery units. In fact, in addition to the personnel who performed essential ground services (airfield services, construction, repair, medical, transport, etc.), the Luftwaffe had three major combat corps: the air force units, the Flak units, and the signals units since, according to contemporary German military thinking, air warfare was not possible without the proper development of these units in all their dimensions.

Let us now return to where we began, to Spain in July 1936. That was the time when Germany must have felt most threatened by its neighbors, who might have been tempted to attack before it developed its military capability to an effective level. Its armed forces, especially the recently formed Luftwaffe, were in the throes of a dizzying expansion process. The decision to support the Spanish anti-communist insurgents was extremely risky and represented, in the best case hypothesis, an added complication.

And yet that was the decision taken. In Spain the Luftwaffe would fight the first round of the battle against communism that it felt was its mission. How that expeditionary combat force, the Legion Condor, functioned is the subject of the following pages.

Diploma
Overleaf. *Unteroffizier der Reserve*, Bernhardt Ritter, the artilleryman to whom this service diploma belongs, served in the General Göring Regiment and in the *Wehrbezirkskommando* (Military Recruiting District) "Berlin X" between April 1936 and October 1938. The regiment which bore the name of the German Air Minister was the embryo of one of the most famous German divisions in World War II.

Der **Uffz. d. Res. Bernhard Ritter**
geb. am 1. September 1913 in Hameln
hat vom 1. April 1936 bis 27. Oktober 1938
beim Regiment General Göring und Wehrbezirkskommando Berlin X
seine aktive Dienstpflicht erfüllt.

Berlin W 15, den 29.10.1938

Der Wehrbezirkskdr.

Major (E)

CHAPTER I

Notes on the German Intervention

When General Franco saw that the civil-military uprising against the *Frente Popular* had partially failed, he realized that he needed to acquire war materiel from abroad to face up to the threat posed by government forces. The most pressing need was for transport aircraft to fly the Army of Africa to the peninsula, fighter planes to protect them, and anti-aircraft artillery to defend the airfields.

In addition to the enquiries made in Italy by emissaries sent by Franco (by the journalist Luis Bolín to be precise) and by other emissaries sent by General Mola, the nationalist leader also wanted to ask for help from Germany, where the regime was profoundly anti-communist.

The key player in obtaining this materiel was the German industrialist, Johannes Bernhardt, resident in Tetuan and economic head of the Foreign Organization of the Nazi Party in Spanish North Africa. It was he who carried the request for aid, drafted personally by Franco as "Commander-in-Chief of the Armed Forces in Morocco," to the German government. He was accompanied on the mission by the head of the National Socialist Party in Morocco, Adolf P. Langenheim, and *Capitán de Aviación* Francisco Arranz, who shortly before had been appointed Chief of the Air Force General Staff in Africa by Franco himself.

Bernhardt
Johannes Eberhard Bernhardt was a German businessman whose contacts with Franco resulted in Germany providing aid to the Nationalists.

Bohle
Right. He was the head in Germany of the *Auslands Organisation*, the Foreign Organization of the Nazi Party.

Letter opener and badge
Bernhardt organized the HISMA, a trading company used to channel all kinds of transactions between the insurgents and Hitler's Germany.

Aboard a Lufthansa Junkers Ju 52 German requisitioned some days earlier in Las Palmas, the commission set off for Germany in the afternoon of July 2. After a meeting and discussions with Rudolf Hess, number two in the NSDAP hierarchy, Hitler received Bernhardt, who carried the weight of the interview since Langenheim stayed in the background and Arranz was not even at the meeting. The encounter took place at Bayreuth, where the *Führer* used to attend the Wagnerian festival held every year on the night of the 25th.

After hearing Bernhardt read out a translation of Franco's missive and asking a number of questions, including some to find out exactly who this unknown Spanish General was, Hitler decided to agree to the request (after receiving information during the interview that the Government in Madrid had already received materiel from France and would soon do so from the Soviet Union as well).

Rudolf Hess
Left. Hitler's right hand man influenced the final decision to help the insurgents.

The aid operation was given the codename "*Unternehmen Feuerzauber*" – Operation Magic Fire.

After several meetings with high-ranking German officers in Berlin to work out the parameters of the aid deal, the commission sent by Franco returned to Tetuan on the 28th with the good news.

Meanwhile, in the capital of the Reich a special section called *Sonderstab W* was set up within the Air Ministry General Staff which would be responsible for planning the implementation of the aid program. *Generalleutnant* Helmuth Wilberg was appointed to lead the section.

On July 29 the first aircraft began to arrive

The Valkyrie
Hitler attended the Bayreuth Festival every year.

Richard Wagner
The German composer was the favorite of the National-Socialist regime.

Notes on the German Intervention

Anti-aircraft guns
The insurgents had an urgent need for transport aircraft, modern fighters and anti-aircraft guns. In the photo, a group of soldiers operate a 20mm Flak 30.

by air from Germany, in the form of nine Junkers Ju 52/3m transport aircraft of a total of twenty aircraft of this type which were earmarked for the aid program. The remainder of the materiel requested by Franco and granted by Hitler (six Heinkel He 51 fighters, ten Junkers Ju 52, twenty 20mm anti-aircraft guns, radio stations, aerial bombs and other miscellaneous materiel), together with pilots and personnel would arrive in Spain by sea in the early hours of August 7. The equipment was shipped aboard the freighter *Usaramo* and Luftwaffe *Major* von Scheele was in charge of the human contingent, a total of ninety-one men including pilots, officers, technicians and interpreters.

After disembarking at Cadiz, the men and the materiel –the latter safely packed in enormous wooden crates – were put on board a special train bound for Seville. The bombers and the fighters were assembled and test flown at the Tablada airfield, and the first fighter entered into service on August 15.

Although at the beginning the new arrivals wanted to look as if they were part of a group of tourists, it was immediately obvious to the citizens of Seville that they were all dressed the same in eye-catching white suits. Little by little the cloak of secrecy which was supposed to surround the operation was lifted and its true purpose became common knowledge.

Almost as soon as they arrived, the Ju 52s entered into service, transporting the various units of the Army of Africa to the mainland. On August 20 the

Sonderstab W
Above. Correspondence with the letterhead and stamp of the Special Staff "Sonderstab W."

Helmuth Wilberg
Right. The man responsible for "Sonderstab W" was a veteran pilot of the First World War.

LEGIÓN CÓNDOR

German three-engined aircraft received to date became "B Wing" of the Nationalist Air Force, all with Spanish aircrews and assigned to bombing enemy positions during the advance of the African columns on Madrid.

The instructions received by the German pilots, of both fighters and bombers, were that they were not to take part in any combat actions, but were to restrict their role to transport missions and the training of Spanish personnel. But on August 13, *Oberleutnant* Rudolf von Moreau, the man in charge of the Ju 52s in Spain, decided (after discussing it with his superior officer, von Scheele, and receiving his approval) to carry out a bombing raid on the Republican battleship *Jaime I* which was at anchor in the bay of Malaga. Two of his three-

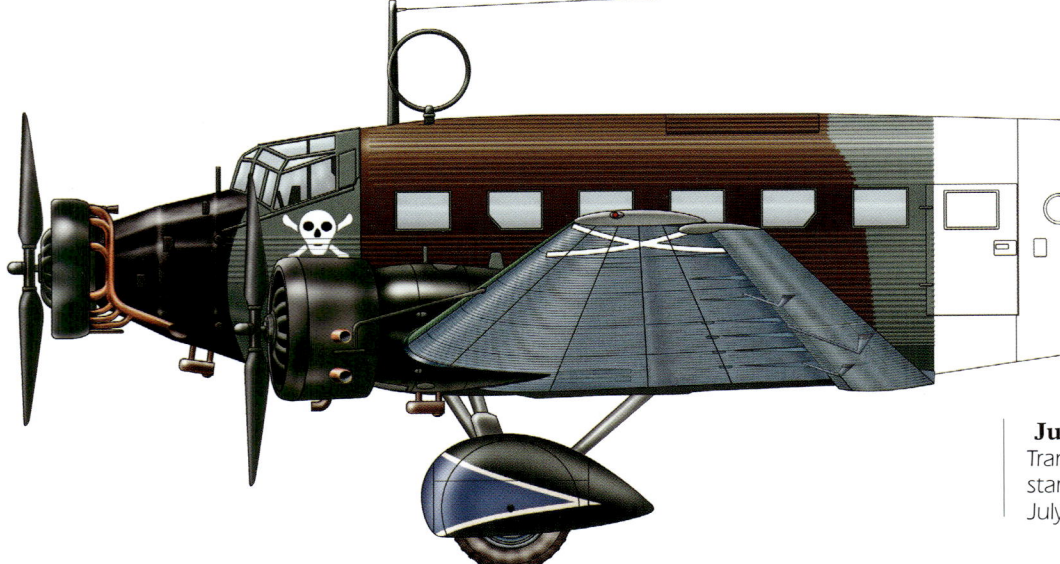

Junkers Ju 52-3mg
Transport aircraft and bomber. They started to arrive in Spain at the end of July 1936.

engined bombers, one of which he piloted himself, dropped a number of bombs on the vessel, only two of which were on target, causing minor damage. This operation was the first German military action in the Spanish civil war.

Rudolf von Moreau
Below. A German pilot, the first commander of Junkers Ju 52s in Spain.

NOTES ON THE GERMAN INTERVENTION

Spanish sojourn
Left. A group of German soldiers, dressed in civilian clothing, photographed on the ship taking them to Spain in August 1936.

Alcázar
Center. Ruins of the Alcázar in Toledo. Its stoic defense was news the world over.

From that date on, the number of combat missions flown by aircraft with German aircrews increased steadily. On August 22 von Moreau himself, running the gauntlet of Republican anti-aircraft fire, flew a couple of missions to drop supplies to the insurgents besieged in the Alcázar in Toledo. On the first run he failed in his attempt, dropping his load outside the confines of the fortress, but on the second he was successful. On the 28th this intrepid pilot made the first air raid on Madrid, bombing the War Ministry building and the *Estación del Norte* railway station.

For their part, the fighter pilots who had come to teach the Spanish pilots to fly the He 51s also received permission to fly combat missions, scoring their first victories over enemy aircraft on August 25.

Battleship
The first act of war by the Germans in Spain was the bombing of the battleship *Jaime I*, an *España* class vessel.

Merchantman
The *St. Louis* was, together with the *Berlin*, the first vessel to transport the He 51s – disguised as farm machinery – which would equip fighter unit of the newly formed Legion Condor. It docked in Cadiz on November 18, 1936.

From mid-August more German aid war materiel began arriving. A succession of freighters docked at insurgent held ports and also at the port of Lisbon, from where the materiel was transported by rail across the border.

Early in September, *Oberstleutnant* Walter Warlimont was sent to Spain to replace von Scheele and serve as a liaison between the Government of the 3rd Reich and the Nationalist authorities. Reports sent by that officer to Berlin had the effect of increasing German aid with shipments of a variety of air force

Heinkel He 51
The first fighter aircraft to be sent to the insurgents by the German government.

Notes on the German Intervention

Warlimont
Staff officer *Oberstleutnant* Walter Warlimont (shown in the photo as a General during World War II) was sent to Spain in September 1936 to replace *Major* von Scheele as head of the German volunteers and to liaise between the Reich and the Nationalist authorities.

materiel and other military supplies, as well as ground materiel – tanks, anti-tank artillery and support vehicles. The latter materiel, destined for the ground forces codenamed *Gruppe Imker* (Beekeeper Group), arrived at the port of Cadiz on October 7. The shipment comprised forty-one Panzer I tanks, twenty-four anti-tank guns, and several trucks for towing guns and carrying ammunition. A total of 267 men made up the human contingent. Throughout the war these ground units would be under the command of *Oberstleutnant* von Funck, although the armored troop component, which came to be known as the *Panzergruppe Drohne* or *Gruppe Thoma* would be under the orders of *Oberstleutnant* Wilhelm *Ritter* von Thoma, who was responsible for their organization.

Panzer I
The first Panzer IA tanks arrived by rail, packed in large wooden crates, at the station of Aldea del Cano, Cáceres, on October 9, 1936.

LEGIÓN CÓNDOR

During the months of September and October the He 51 fighters piloted by Germans scored a considerable number of victories, which shows how well trained these pilots were. Similarly, on the ground, the Panzer I tanks notched up their first success on October 25 when they captured the village of Villamantilla, near the town of Navalcarnero, during the Nationalist Army's advance on Madrid.

Drohne
Top. Two members of the *Drohne* Group look at 37mm anti-tank gun. As can be seen by their clothing, this photo was taken shortly after their arrival in Spain, since neither of them is in uniform.

Von Funck
Right. The Arguijuelas castles, Cáceres, the first base of the German tank unit volunteers. Looking out over its battlements we see *Oberstleutnant* von Funck, head of the German ground forces in Spain, known as the *Imker* Group, accompanied by one of the German interpreters, Vollrath.

NOTES ON THE GERMAN INTERVENTION

Light tank
Above. The Panzerkampfwagen I Ausf.A was the most common armored vehicle to be sent to Spain by the Germans during the Spanish Civil War.

Ornamentation
Center. Paperweight of the period, representing a Panzer I Ausf.A.

Von Thoma
Previous page, center. *Oberstleutnant* von Thoma, wearing a black beret, commanded the German armored forces in Spain, seen here accompanied by a Spanish *Alférez* (Lieutenant) with a number of Spanish soldiers in October 1936.

Plaque
Left. A German plaque from 1936 of the 1st Panzer Regiment.

The formation of the Legion Condor

Late in October, the head of the German military secret service, *Admiral* Wilhelm Canaris, was commissioned by Hitler to hold talks with Franco and offer him more aid, both human and material, to counteract the aid provided to the Republic by the Soviet Union and France, mainly, which was growing with every passing day. The outcome of the talks, which took place at Franco's HQ in Salamanca, was the formation of a unit to be commanded by a German officer who would be subordinate only to Franco himself.

This unit, made up of volunteer military personnel, mainly drawn from the air force although there would also be army and navy contingents, was officially formed on October 30 and would be known as the "Legion Condor." Its organization and transport to Spain would be the responsibility of *Sonderstab W*, the special Staff, which had hitherto been in charge of all the logistics of German aid since August. The codename of this operation would be *"Winterübung Rügen"* or "Winter exercise on the Isle of Rügen."

Adolf Hitler
After his meeting with Johannes Bernhardt, Hitler gave the go ahead for German intervention in the Spanish Civil War.

Volunteers
Over page, below. The first German contingent, comprising nearly 700 volunteers, would arrive at Seville on November 16, 1936 aboard the merchantman *Fulda*.

Francisco Franco
On October 1, 1936, Franco was proclaimed *Generalísimo* of the Nationalist Army.

Sperrle
Generalmajor Sperrle was the first commander in chief of the Legion Condor.

The first contingent of the new unit embarked at the German port of Stettin aboard the freighter *Fulda* on November 6, just six days after its official formation, which gives an idea of the speed with which the German military authorities formed the unit. On the 16th the vessel sailed up the Guadalquivir to arrive at Seville, and the 697 volunteers dressed in civilian clothing immediately went ashore

To lead the Legion Condor, Berlin appointed *Generalmajor* Hugo Sperrle, who would have *Oberstleutnant* Alexander Holle as his Chief of General Staff until January 20, 1937 when Holle was relieved by *Oberst* Wolfram *Freiherr* von Richthofen.

For organizational purposes the Luftwaffe assigned number 88 to the volunteer unit and divided the its troops into the following units:

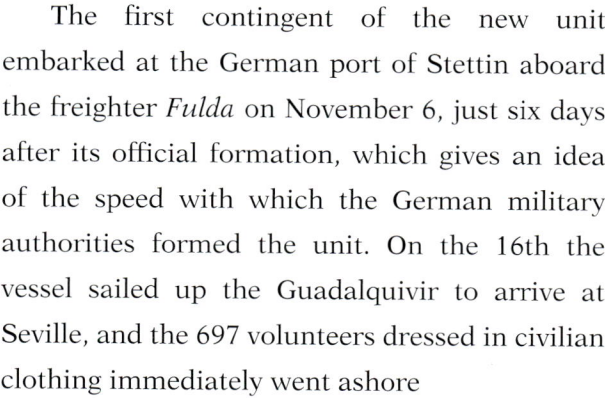

ORGANIZATION OF THE LEGION CONDOR

Führungsstab: S/88 (High Command, General Staff and corresponding services).

Kampfgruppe: K/88 (Bomber Group, with 3 squadrons of 12 aircraft; in April 1937 a 4th squadron was formed, called *Versuchsbomberstaffel* or Experimental Bomber Squadron).

Jagdgruppe: J/88 (Fighter Group, with 4 squadrons of 12 aircraft; the 4th squadron was disbanded during the war).

Aufklärungsstaffel: A/88 (Reconnaissance Squadron, with 12 aircraft).

Gemischte Aufklärungs und Bombenstaffel (See), AS/88 (Mixed Naval Reconnaissance and Bombing Squadron, with 6 seaplanes).

Luftnachrichten-Abteilung (mot.): Ln/88 (Motorized Signals Battalion, comprising 4 companies, one Radio, one Telephone, one Air Communications and one Air Warning).

Flak-Abteilung (mot.): F/88 (Motorized Anti-Aircraft Battalion, which was initially composed of one light 20mm battery and one heavy 88mm battery, but later, at the end of 1936, comprised two 20mm batteries and four – five as from 1938 – 88mm batteries, as well as one ammunition battery, one searchlight and sound locator battery and one battery for training Spanish recruits).

Luftzeuggruppe und Luftpark: P/88 (Air Maintenance Group and Depot), whose mission was to maintain air materiel and, when necessary, try to salvage aircraft damaged for any reason).

Munitions-Anstalt: MA/88 (Ammunition Disbursement).

Sanitäts-Abteilung: San/88 (Medical Battalion).

Lazarett: Laz/88 (Field Hospital; a number of field hospitals were set up at various locations in Nationalist held Spain).

Wetterstelle: W/88 (Weather Unit).

Versuchsjagdstaffel: VJ/88 (Experimental Fighter Squadron; officially formed early in 1937).

Versuchsbomberstaffel: VB/88 (Experimental Bomber Squadron; formed in February 1937).

Verbindungsstab: VS/88 (Liaison Office to liaise with Italian and Spanish air forces).

Büro Grau: (Grey Department; Office of the Air Attaché).

Büro Anker: (Anchor Department, Office of the Naval Attaché).

Imker-Gruppe: ("Beekeeper" Group) a group of volunteers from the German ground forces, composed of the *Imker-Drohne* tank group, which included two companies of tank – at the end of December 1937 a third was formed –, one transport company, one repair company and support unit, a 37mm anti-tank guns unit, a depot and spares unit – established in Valladolid – and a little later a tank and anti-tank gun school was set up at Cubas de la Sagra in the province of Madrid, once it had been captured; *Imker-Ausbilder*, a group of trainers from various corps teaching in Spanish military academies; and *Imker-Horch*, a radio-interception company).

Gruppe Nordsee: (North Sea Group, comprising officers and specialists from the *Kriegsmarine* with an advisory and instruction role within Nationalist navy units and at a number of ports on the coast of Nationalist held territory).

Legion Condor

Heinkel 51
Above, left. Initially these aircraft equipped Group J/88.

Junkers 52
Above, right. Transport and bomber.

The Legion Condor was equipped with the following materiel:

- **Heinkel He 51 B**: fighters which, together with those previously sent from Germany, formed Group J/88; they were later to be replaced by Bf 109s.

- **Junkers Ju 52/3mg 3e & 4e**: used as bombers and transport aircraft by Group K/88.

- **Bf 109** (various prototypes): fighter aircraft sent to be tested in actual combat situations (one of them, coded V-4, was destroyed on its maiden flight on December 10, 1936 when it crashed after suffering an engine failure. V-3 was tested and some minor faults were detected, although it would later see combat as part of VJ/88).

Prototype
Tablada Airfield, Seville, December 1936. Bf 109 V.3 piloted by *Hauptmann* Trautloft, whose personal motif – a green heart – can be seen on the side of the cockpit. This was the first aircraft of this type to arrive in Spain and it was coded 6-1.

NOTES ON THE GERMAN INTERVENTION

HEINKEL HE 46 C: high-wing monoplanes for close reconnaissance and support roles. They were nicknamed *"Pava"* (Turkey Hen) and were delivered straight to the Nationalist Air Force without ever forming part of the Legion Condor.

HEINKEL HE 45: biplanes used in a tactical reconnaissance and artillery spotting role, which formed part of A/88 squadron. They were known by the nickname *"Pavo"* (Turkey Cock).

Heinkel 45
Above. He 45 at the El Burgo de Osma airfield in Soria.

Bf 109 V-3
The first Messerschmitt Bf 109 used in Spain.

Heinkel 70
Below. One of the fastest aircraft of the Luftwaffe at that time.

Legion Condor

Heinkel He 60
Right. The first German seaplanes to arrive in Spain, in 1936.

Rayo
Center. The He 70 monoplanes were the first strategic reconnaissance aircraft to be used in Spain.

Heinkel He 59
Below. These twin-engined seaplanes made up the backbone of the Legion Condor's marine reconnaissance unit.

Notes on the German Intervention

Heinkel He 50 G: dive-bombing biplane of which only one example was sent for testing. The aircraft was probably sent back to Germany after its poor performance in Spanish skies.

Heinkel He 50 G
Above. Its time in Spain was fleeting.

Heinkel He 60 E: sea biplanes fitted with a two-bladed fixed-pitch wooden propeller which flew in the German AS/88 squadron.

Heinkel He 70 E & F: long-range reconnaissance and light bombers, nicknamed "*Rayo*" (Lightning), which flew in A/88 squadron until they were transferred to the Nationalist Air Force in October 1937.

Heinkel He 112 V-5
Center. This monoplane fighter was called the "*Kanonenvogel*" (Cannon-bird).

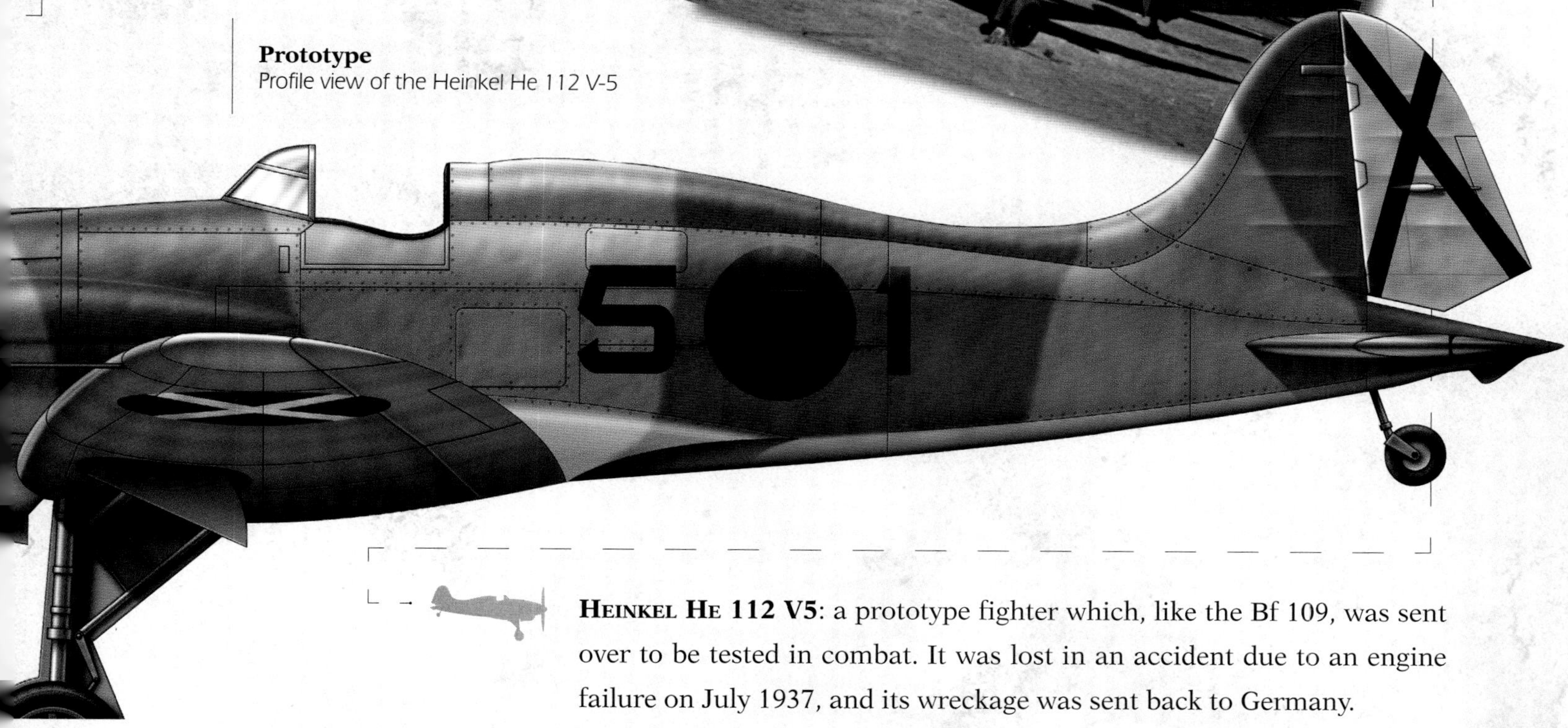

Heinkel He 59 B-2: twin-engined sea biplanes which operated as part of AS/88. They were known as "*Zapatones*" (Big Shoes) because of their large floats.

Prototype
Profile view of the Heinkel He 112 V-5

Heinkel He 112 V5: a prototype fighter which, like the Bf 109, was sent over to be tested in combat. It was lost in an accident due to an engine failure on July 1937, and its wreckage was sent back to Germany.

Henschel Hs 123
Above. The first such machine to arrive in Spain, hence its strange numbering.

Junkers W 34
Center. The photo shows the first one sent to the Legion Condor.

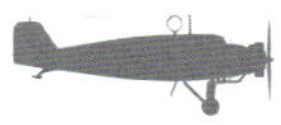

JUNKERS W 34 HI: used in Spain as weather, liaison and transport aircraft. They operated as part of Bomber Group K/88 and in the S/88 Command Unit.

HENSCHEL HS 123 A-1: dive-bombing and tactical support biplanes tested in the VJ/88 (experimental fighter squadron) after October 1936, which were later to be transferred to the "*Stuka 88,*" experimental unit, before the surviving aircraft were finally handed over to the Nationalist Air Force. They were known by the nickname of "*Angelito*" (Little Angel).

 **Junkers Ju 87 V-4**: a dive-bomber prototype known as the "*Stuka*" which arrived in Spain (a single machine in November 1936), like other types of aircraft, to be tested under real combat conditions. Operating as part of VJ/88 squadron, it saw action in Andalusia and in the Center under conditions of absolute secrecy. In January 1937 the aircraft was loaded onto a vessel in Vigo and returned to Germany as surreptitiously as it had arrived and had flown in the months it was operational in Spain.

Stuka prototype
Center. The D-UBIP was the prototype V-4 Junkers Ju 87 which was sent to Spain for testing.

With regard to ground units – including those under air command but operating on the ground – which had already been serving prior to the formation of the Legion Condor, all their personnel together with their corresponding materiel (tanks, artillery batteries, vehicles) were incorporated into the Legion once it was officially formed. Considering only major elements, this materiel was as follows:

Panzerkampfwagen I Ausf.A: light tanks equipping *Panzergruppe Drohne*. They were poorly armed and their armor left much to be desired. They were training tanks.

Panzer
Below. These were sent to the *Gruppe Drohne* to train Spanish tank crews.

LEGION CONDOR

PaK 35/36: 37mm anti-tank gun. They were not bad guns at the time, although they would soon be rendered obsolete.

Flak 30: 20mm light anti-aircraft cannon which, as from November 1936 equipped two batteries of Group F/88.

Flak 18: 88mm heavy anti-aircraft cannon which, as from November 1936, equipped four batteries of the Legion Condor's anti-aircraft group.

Light anti-aircraft
Above. 20mm anti-aircraft gun during the event held at Sanjurjo Airfield, Zaragoza on March 1, 1939.

Anti-tank cannon
Above, right. Several camouflaged 37mm anti-tank cannon with their towing vehicles in Alar del Rey, Palencia.

"Eighty-eight"
Left. 88mm cannon emplacement to provide anti-aircraft protection for the La Cenia airfield, Tarragona.

Notes on the German Intervention

As the war progressed, new materiel arrived for the various German air and ground units, either complementing what they already had or replacing some of the equipment types.

This materiel was as follows:

Arado Ar 95 A-0: reconnaissance and attack seaplane which was received when the Spanish civil war was already over. The Legion Condor's seaplane squadron was transferred immediately to the new Spanish Air Force.

Arado Ar 68 E-1: experimental biplane night-fighters which failed to meet the requirements expected of them due to their poor performance and were consequently used for ground attack missions.

Seaplanes
Above. Pollensa base. Two Ar 95s, two He 60s (one without wings, in the background) and one Italian Cant Z-501.

Arado 68
Center. Two Ar 68 E.1 fighters among the olive trees at La Cenia airfield.

Dornier Do 17
Do 17 in flight over the operations zone.

DORNIER DO 17 E, F & P: used for long-range reconnaissance and bombing missions, nicknamed *"Bacalao"* (Cod). They were first assigned to VB/88 and then all the various versions received were transferred to A/88.

HEINKEL HE 111 B-1, E-1 & E-3: twin-engined bombers nicknamed *"Pedro."* At first they formed part of VB/88 before being transferred later to K/88.

Heinkel He 111
Center. He 111 of the 3.K/88 at the Zaragoza airfield. 1938.

FIESELER FI 156 A-1: light aircraft for observation and personnel transport nicknamed *"Cigüeña,"* from their German name, *Storch* (English: Stork). They were used by S/88 and P/88.

Fieseler Fi 156
Right. "Storch" liaison aircraft.

Notes on the German Intervention

Heinkel He 115
Base at Pollensa, Mallorca. One of the two seaplanes He 115 delivered for testing.

Bacalao
Center. Profile view of a Dornier Do 17 of Group A/88.

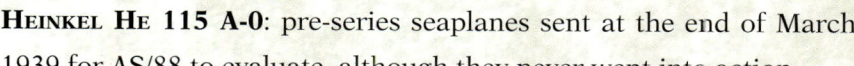
HEINKEL HE 115 A-0: pre-series seaplanes sent at the end of March 1939 for AS/88 to evaluate, although they never went into action.

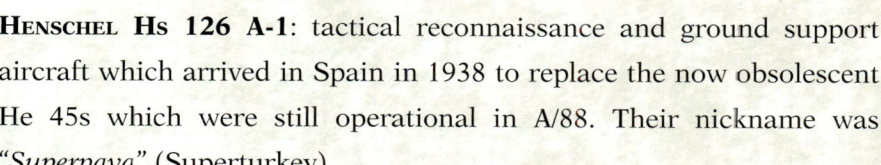

HENSCHEL HS 126 A-1: tactical reconnaissance and ground support aircraft which arrived in Spain in 1938 to replace the now obsolescent He 45s which were still operational in A/88. Their nickname was *"Superpava"* (Superturkey).

Henschel Hs 126
Right. The aircraft in the photo is at the Zaragoza airfield during the event held on March 1, 1939.

Legion Condor

JUNKERS JU 52-3MG SEE: a seaplane version of the multipurpose three-engined aircraft; it was assigned to AS/88.

Three-engined seaplane
Above, left. Ju 52-3mg See at Pollensa.

JUNKERS JU 86 D-1: twin-engined bombers assigned to VB/88 to be tested in action. They were known by the nickname "*Jumo*."

Jumo
Above, right. Ju 86D-1. The frequent technical problems suffered by these aircraft meant that they were only a short time in service with the Legion Condor.

KLEMM KL 32A.XIV: light aircraft used for personnel transport and liaison missions by S/88.

JUNKERS JU 87 A & B: dive-bombers. The first aircraft of these series arrived towards the end of 1937 in the case of the A-1, and at the end of 1938 in the case of the B-1.

Junkers
Below, right. Ju 87B at the La Cenia airfield.

Klemm Kl 32a
Below, left. One of the four three-seater light aircraft Kl 32a.XIV that came to Spain in early-1937.

NOTES ON THE GERMAN INTERVENTION

Taifun
Right. Zaragoza airfield, Bf 108B of K/88, used as a mail carrier.

MESSERSCHMITT BF 108 B: liaison and light transport monoplanes also used by S/88. Their nickname was *"Taifun"* (Typhoon).

Model
A good reproduction of a Heinkel 111 in the livery of the Luftwaffe, made in the 1930s.

MESSERSCHMITT BF 109 B, C, D & E: excellent fighters which arrived after the V-3 and V-4 prototypes (a third prototype, the V-5, arrived in January 1937) and equipped squadrons of Group J/88, replacing the Heinkel He 51.

Messer
Below. The Bf 109 B-1 began to arrive in Spain in January 1937.

Prototype
Left. April 1938. He 112 V.9 flown by *Hauptmann* Harder. Previously this aircraft had been flown by *Oberleutnants* Radusch and Balthasar and by *Unteroffizier* Schulz.

 HEINKEL HE 112 V-8 & V-9: new prototypes of this fighter which did not actually ever form part of the Legion Condor since they were sent back to Germany after being evaluated by Spanish pilots.

 PANZERKAMPFWAGEN I AUSF.B: light tanks equipped with a more powerful engine than the previous version, the Ausf.A.

 **FLAK 18, mod. 1935**: 37mm anti-aircraft cannons assigned to Group F/88 to equip its light batteries.

Light tank
Center, right. The Panzer I Ausf.B was a little more maneuverable than its brother, the Ausf.B. In color, the front panel of a tank in service with the Spanish army.

Flak 18
Below. Flak 18 was the name given not only to the 37mm anti-aircraft machine gun shown here but also its big brother, the 88mm cannon.

Badge
Above, right. The *Zylinder Hut* (Top Hat) emblem of Squadron 2.J/88.

Mickey Mouse
Center. Emblem of Squadron 3.J/88, painted on some of the He 51s of that squadron. Later, for the Bf 109, a different version of the popular mouse was used.

At first the new units (which were joined by the German troops who had arrived in Spain prior to the official formation of the Legion Condor) were stationed at the following locations:

The first three squadrons of Group K/88, at the Tablada airfield, near Seville, shortly to be moved to the San Fernando airfield in Salamanca.

The 1st Squadron of Group J/88 – 1.J/88 – called "*Marabú*" (Giant Stork), at the Virgen del Camino airfield in Leon.

The 2nd Squadron of Group J/88 – 2.J/88 – called "*Sombrero de Copa*" (Top Hat), at the Lacua airfield, Vitoria.

The 3rd Squadron of Group J/88 – 3.J/88 – known as "Mickey Mouse," at the Escalona del Prado airfield in Toledo.

The 4th Squadron of Group J/88 – 4.J/88 – called "*As de Picas*" (Ace of Spades), the last one to be formed, at the Avila airfield.

A/88 squadron was based at Avila, and later at Seville, although its aircraft also flew out of other airfields.

Biplane fighter
The Fighter Group of the Legion Condor was initially equipped with He 51 biplanes.

The Command Unit, S/88 and the Depot, P/88, were located at Avila.

AS/88 was first stationed at the Puntales naval base in Cadiz, before moving to the El Atalayón seaplane base in Melilla, and later to Pollensa (the Balearics).

Part of the F/88 anti-aircraft group – two 88mm heavy batteries – remained at the Tablada air base in Seville to protect it. Another part of F/88 – three 88mm heavy batteries and two 20mm light batteries – was sent to the Madrid front.

The tank and anti-tank artillery units were sent to the castles at Arguijuelas (Cáceres) where Spanish personnel were already being trained as tank crews and artillerymen. Later, the headquarters of the *Panzergruppe Drohne* was set up in the village of Cubas de la Sagra (Madrid) while the training centers were at Oropesa (Toledo) and Casarrubuelos (Madrid) for tank crews, and at Carranque and Cedillo for anti-tank personnel.

These were the main bases used, although in the early stages of the official German intervention (between mid-November 1936 and March 20, 1937, the date on which the Legion Condor was reorganized), some of the air force formations were obliged to be constantly on the move as they used the nearest airfields to whichever battle fronts were active at the time (Central, North, Andalusia and Aragon).

Hotel
The Hotel Cristina in Seville, in which German volunteers set up their headquarters in Spain in September 1936, before the formation of the Legion Condor.

Arguijuelas
In October 1936 the headquarters of the *Panzergruppe Drohne* was located in the Arguijuelas castles (two separate structures called the Upper and Lower Castles), some 14km from the city of Cáceres.

FIRST MILITARY OPERATIONS OF THE LEGION CONDOR.

On November 18 the Madrid front was the scene of the first combat actions carried out by the Ju 52s of K/88 squadron, which bombed a number of military targets in the vicinity of the capital. In the following days these same aircraft would fly more sorties against enemy positions.

About the same time the first dogfights between Group J/88 fighters and Republican aircraft were fought in the sky over Madrid, resulting in a number of government aircraft being shot down with no German losses. As for the Reconnaissance Squadron (A/88), its aircraft had already carried out missions over this front earlier in the month.

With regard to ground operations, Panzer I engaged Soviet T-26B tanks in the Humera-Pozuelo sector. The Russian tanks, superior in all aspects to the German machines, easily halted the German advance.

Early in December the first prototypes of the Messerschmitt Bf 109 and the Heinkel He 112 to arrive in Spain flew over this Central front.

But these missions over the Madrid front were not the first nor the only missions to be flown by Legion Condor aircraft, since in mid-November several Ju 52s had bombed the Mediterranean ports of Alicante and Cartagena. These

City walls
Above. Members of *Panzergruppe Drohne* at the foot of Avila's city walls.

Documentation
Spanish military ID card of German sergeant of the Motorized Anti-Aircraft Battalion (F/88). Notice that nowhere does the nationality of the holder appear and that his first name has been "Hispanicized."

Russian tank
The first armored engagements in the Spanish Civil War demonstrated the superiority of the Soviet materiel over the German.

were both strategic points where, at this stage in the war, Soviet vessels were still docking with supplies and war materiel for the Republican army. In another theater of operations, in Andalusia, where there was a certain amount of activity in some sectors, Legion Condor aircraft flew numerous missions, among the most important of which was deliver supplies to the besieged *Santa María de la Cabeza* monastery between late November and May 2, 1937 when it finally fell into enemy hands.

On the Northern front, air operations were also carried out involving Legion Condor aircraft, between the end of November 1936 and the first months of 1937. Heinkel He 51 fighters engaged enemy aircraft in a great many dogfights while the three-engined bombers of K/88 flew bombing sorties, mainly over the provinces of Vizcaya and Santander.

The first major battles in the Spanish civil war did not take place until 1937 and, naturally, Legion Condor aircraft were involved. The cutting of the Coruña road and the Battle of Jarama were the most important actions on the Central front in the first months of the year and German fighters and bombers played a leading role. They also cooperated in the protection

First flights
He 112 V.5 coded 5•1 at the Tablada airfield.

Notes on the German Intervention

Unteroffizier
Photo of a member of the Legion Condor with his rank badge.

of withdrawing Italian units after the Battle of Guadalajara in March. The artillery units of F/88 also provided their firepower in these operations.

On the Southern front, the He 59s and He 60s of AS/88 supported the Nationalist advance through the province of Malaga which began in m i d - January and concluded with the capture of the city of Malaga on February 8. Meanwhile, in mid-February, He 70s of A/88 Squadron carried out successful raids on the hydroelectric power plants at Tremp and Balaguer, situated in the Pyrenees and vital to Catalonian industry.

Three-engined aircraft
Most of the aircraft to attack the town of Guernica were Junkers Ju 52s.

RESTRUCTURING OF THE UNIT AND NORTHERN CAMPAIGN

At the end of March, taking advantage of a lull in military operations, the air arm of the Legion Condor was restructured with the incorporation of the new aircraft received since January: Messerschmitt Bf 109 B-1, Heinkel He 111, Dornier Do 17 F-1, and Junkers Ju 86 D.

Due to the start of the offensive in the north, late in March most of the German units (a total of eighty-five aircraft) moved to that front, setting up bases at Burgos and Vitoria.

Oberst von Richthofen, Chief of General Staff of the Legion Condor at that time, who had been appointed chief of air operations on the Northern front by the Nationalist high command, set up his center of operations in Vitoria from where he would plan the actions of all three air forces (Italian, German and Spanish) in the area during the months that the campaign lasted.

As from the last day of March, the day the Vizcaya campaign started, the German air force units, in cooperation with Spanish and Italian units, threw everything they had against the enemy's defensive positions in the province and against its capital city, Bilbao, and fighters Group J/88 engaged in dogfights with the few aircraft that the Government of Euzkadi could muster. In the skies over the Basque Country the Nationalist Air Force enjoyed total supremacy.

Airfield
Above. The Czech aircraft Aero A-101 shared airfield with units of the Legion Condor in the north.

Formation
Below. A formation of Ju 52s flying over Burgos. German bomber squadrons operated regularly out of Burgos airfield during the Northern campaign.

Notes on the German Intervention

During this campaign, the event for which the German participation in the Spanish civil war is best known occurred: the bombing of the town of Guernica. On the back of lies and propagandistic distortions, this event, which took place on April 26, 1937, has become an indictment against the Legion Condor. In the afternoon of that day the emblematic town, of undeniable strategic and military importance, was bombed, not as a center of population as such, but because it represented a vital communications node. The main elements of this node were the bridge over the river Oca, which was being used by retreating Republican units as it was the only one linking the Basque positions in the south with their rearguard, and the confluence of roads from the east that was some 200 meters before the bridge.

Ruins of Guernica
Above. The bombing of the emblematic Basque town triggered a virulent press campaign against the German forces.

Pamphlet
The Basque government made intelligent use of propaganda in defense of their interests.

Cartoon
Right. Black humor was also used with regard to the bombing of Guernica.

Therefore, the destruction of the bridge would have the effect of trapping a large enemy force. Consequently, the objectives were of a strictly military nature and the action cannot be seen in any way as the bombing of civilian targets of no importance to military operations.

In succession, three Italian Savoia SM.79s, one German Dornier Do 17, one (or two according to some sources, although this has not been conclusively proved) Heinkel He 111s, also German, and nineteen Ju 52s – which were undoubtedly the ones which caused the most damage – dropped their bombs on the crucial bridge, which for a number of reasons was not hit.

Savoia bomber
Above. Italian Savoia SM.79 bombers began the bombing raid against bridge at Guernica.

Book
Center. A British publication that exaggerated the bombing of Guernica.

VB/88
Below. Heinkel He 111s of the experimental unit also attacked Guernica.

NOTES ON THE GERMAN INTERVENTION

Lauburu
Right. The Basque cross, often used by the Basque Nationalist *Gudaris* (soldiers), was very reminiscent of the swastika.

25% of the buildings of the town were totally destroyed by the bombs, a percentage which rose to 70% due to the subsequent fires. According to the most recent studies, the number of fatal victims was no higher than 126.

Throughout the campaign, aircraft from K/88, J/88 and A/88 made a large number of raids on enemy fortifications –including those known as the "Iron Belt" – and on other positions and troop concentrations until the end of the campaign on June 30, 1937.

Regulations
Regulations book of the Popular Republican Army.

Paper money
Five peseta bill issued in Bilbao in January 1937.

Iron Belt
Below. Concrete fortifications near Bilbao.

NOTES ON THE GERMAN INTERVENTION

Ruins
Previous page. The war was leaving its mark in various towns in Vizcaya.

Iron Belt
The defenders of Vizcaya believed the defenses of the pompously named Iron Belt to be impenetrable. Reality showed just how wrong they were.

Legion Condor

BATTLE OF BRUNETE AND END OF THE NORTHERN CAMPAIGN

Early in July, action on the Northern front ground to a halt due to the start of a strong offensive unleashed by the Popular Army on the Madrid front. This offensive, which led to what we now call the "Battle of Brunete," started in the early hours of July 6. The intention was to cut off the Nationalist forces surrounding the Spanish capital and also to draw troops away from operations in the North.

Air and ground units of the Legion Condor (as well as several other Nationalist Army units) were urgently moved from one front to the other and, as early as the 7th, German aircraft began to operate against the enemy in the sector. Responsibility for air operations was entrusted to *General* Sperrle who, despite being outnumbered by the Republicans in terms of aircraft, succeeded in ruling the skies over the front. By July 26 the battle could be said to be over, after which the men and equipment of the Legion Condor were sent back to the Northern front, where by mid-August the offensive that had been halted at the beginning of the previous month was once again set in motion. About eighty German aircraft, numerous tanks and several Flak units were involved in the offensive and by the end of August the occupation of the province of Santander had been completed.

Without giving respite to the enemy, the Nationalist troops entered Asturias, where they faced stronger resistance than they had encountered in either

Soviet tank
Above. The Popular Army had the most modern tanks of the time. In the photo, a T-26.

Helmet
French type used by a combatant of the International Brigades.

Propaganda
Propaganda played a key role throughout the conflict

of the other two northern provinces captured previously. The weight of air operations was borne on this occasion by the aircraft of the Legion Condor. Between fighters, bombers and reconnaissance aircraft over ninety aircraft were deployed and a large number of sorties were flown.

Medal
Previous page, center. A commemorative medal of the German unit.

Sperrle
Below. The German general left Spain at the end of the Northern Campaign, receiving the *Medalla Militar Individual* for his services.

SECOND REORGANIZATION AND PARTICIPATION IN THE BATTLE OF TERUEL

Coinciding with the end of the Northern campaign, many Legion Condor personnel were relieved and some of the equipment that they had been using until then was upgraded. These changes mainly affected the air force units.

As part of this reshuffle, *General* Sperrle and his Chief of General Staff, *Oberst* von Richthofen, were replaced by *Generalmajor* Helmuth Volkmann and *Oberstleutnant* Hermann Plocher, respectively.

Midway through December 1937, the Republican army launched a major offensive on the city of Teruel, which on January 8 they succeeded in capturing after overcoming strong and obstinate resistance from its defenders. The

Inspection
Above. *General* Gil Yuste, commander of the 5th Division (Zaragoza), visiting the La Cenia airfield.

Nationalist counter-offensive had begun on December 29 but had to be called off a few days later due to the harsh weather conditions. The aircraft of the Legion Condor, which were also involved in the fighting, could not take off from their bases until the storm abated several days later. Meanwhile, on the ground, vehicles and artillery pieces were also affected by the low temperatures that rendered them temporarily unserviceable.

In the weeks to follow, with the weather now more amenable, the German fighters and bombers flew a number of missions with great success, as they

Teruel
Teruel was the only provincial capital to fall into Republican hands during the Civil War. In the photo we can see the *Comandancia Militar* (Military Headquarters) and nearby buildings after the fighting.

Stairway and Seminary
The Nationalist defenders of Teruel heroically resisted inside the *Comandancia Militar* and in the seminary building, which ended up totally destroyed. On the left, a photo of Teruel's pretty Mudejar stairway, in which the damage to nearby

also did in the next phase of the counter-offensive, known as the Battle of Alfambra, in which Nationalist troops advanced towards the river of the same name.

As from February 7 three Ju 87 A-1 Stukas began to operate in the sector, having been sent to Spain late the previous year. They formed an independent squadron, initially as part of the J/88 Fighter Group, of which it would become its 5th squadron (5.J/88). These aircraft made successful attacks against tanks and anti-aircraft guns deployed by the Republicans, as well as against various troop concentrations.

Medals
Above. *Medalla de Sufrimientos por la Patria* (Patriotic Suffering Medal) belonging to a German soldier of the Legion.
Below. Award certificate of a Campaign Medal to a German soldier.

Anti-aircraft cannon
75/36mm German Flak gun in a frozen Teruel landscape.

Legion Condor

Stuka
The legendary Junkers Ju 87A made their debut during the Battle of Alfambra.

Belchite
Over page. The ruins of the devastated village of Belchite are preserved today in memory of the tragic battle that took place there.

NOTES ON THE GERMAN INTERVENTION

Das Kloster von Belchite
Hier habe ich mich noch mit einem
Mönch unterhalten, er wollte dort

BATTLE OF THE EBRO AND THE THIRD GREAT REORGANIZATION

After the Republicans made a surprise crossing of the Ebro in the early hours July 25, 1938, with the strategic intention of delaying the collapse of the Levante front and thereby preventing Valencia from falling into Nationalist hands, Legion Condor units cooperated from the first days in the efforts to halt the enemy advance by heavily bombing enemy positions, Mediterranean ports, airfields and the communications nodes of the Republican rearguard. These operations were carried out by aircraft belonging to Group K/88 and A/88 Squadron, although the seaplanes of AS/88 Squadron also took part in the raids. As for the fighters, the Bf 109s were frenetically active, strafing the enemy's defensive positions in the territory they had gained.

Souvenir
Above, left. Detail of key ring type souvenir commemorating Group F/88 of the Legion Condor.

Rifleman
Above, right. Spanish soldier crossing a pontoon bridge over the Ebro.

Lookout post
Members of the Legion Condor observing enemy positions.

Notes on the German Intervention

Taking a break
Above, left. A German soldier reads the paper in the shade of an olive tree at La Cenia.

Zaragoza
Above, right. The Sanjurjo airfield was home to the He 111 bombers of K/88.

Bombs
Below, right. Three Civil Guards pose next to a 500 kilo German bomb.

The Fighter Group (J/88) took over the airfield at La Cenia (Tarragona), while the bombers (K/88) were based at the Sanjurjo airfield (Zaragoza) and the reconnaissance squadron (A/88) was split between Buñuel (Navarra) and Tauste (Zaragoza).

As had occurred during the recent Levante campaign with the Bomber Group, Group J/88 was now assigned a number of Spanish fighter pilots as reinforcements and to enable them to familiarize themselves with the aircraft that would shortly be handed over to Nationalist Air Force. Dogfights between the pilots of the opposing air forces became a regular feature of this long and bloody Battle of the Ebro, each air force fielding the latest models of the fighters received: the Messerschmitt Bf 109 C and D versus the Polikarpov I-16.

The balance was tipped in favor of the German aircraft, although success was not achieved without a cost. In spite of the severe attrition losses the unit as a whole had been suffering in recent months, which by the summer of 1938 had started to be cause for concern, Germany was not replacing lost materiel, since relations with the Spanish authorities were somewhat strained due to differences of opinion over economic matters.

Once these differences were resolved, new air and ground materiel arrived in Spain to reequip the various units, for which equipment levels returned to normal once again.

Late in September there was another major relief of troops and officers in the Legion Condor. On November 1, 1938, Von Richthofen, recently promoted to *Generalmajor* and formerly Chief of General Staff of the Legion Condor under Sperrle, replaced *General* Volkmann as commander-in-chief of the unit with *Oberstleutnant* Hans Seidemann as his Chief of General Staff.

Field kitchen
One of the most important logistical tasks is always to keep the troops fed.

Graffiti
The walls of many Spanish towns and villages were covered with political and military graffiti.

Ammunition
Above. Aviation bombs were stacked ready for immediate use in sorties as shown in the photo.

Cigarette case
Above, right. Toledo handicraft for the German combatants.

Prisoners
Republican troops surrender to the victors.

THE CATALONIAN CAMPAIGN AND THE END OF THE WAR

With the Battle of the Ebro successfully concluded, the Nationalist commanders took another step forward to winning the war. On December 23, 1938 the Catalonia offensive was launched with the aim of reaching the Pyrenees and gaining control over this important region.

The fighters engaged with what was left of the Republican air force and destroyed a large number of enemy aircraft on the ground during attacks on various airfields of the region's three provinces. Meanwhile the seaplanes of

Bullfighting
Ticket for a bullfight held in Zaragoza during the Pilar Festival of 1938. The Germans were strongly drawn to this traditional Spanish spectacle.

AS/88 carried out a number of bombing raids on the ports of Barcelona and Tarragona.

Once the Catalonian campaign was over, the aircraft of the Legion Condor were stationed at the airfields at Avila, Escalona, Barcience-Torrijos, Salamanca and Leon, in preparation for the final offensive.

Parade
Above. *General* von Richthofen reviews Legion Condor troops formed up in Zaragoza at the Sanjurjo airfield in front of He 111 aircraft.

Reconnaissance aircraft
Right. Several aircraft belonging to A/88 in the parade held at Barajas in May 1939.

Barajas
Below. Nearly 500 hundred aircraft were assembled for the Barajas air parade.

NOTES ON THE GERMAN INTERVENTION

Medal award ceremony
Above. At Barajas airport, Franco, in an air force uniform, awards the *Medalla Militar Individual* to a member of the Legion Condor.

In the last weeks of the war several bombing raids were carried out against enemy positions and rearguard. In the Toledo sector, when the final push had already begun, *Oberleutnant* von Bonin, squadron leader of 3.J/88, scored the last victory for the unit, although according to other sources, he had scored this kill, an I-15, on March 6 over Alicante. It was the 314th victory of Fighter Group J/88.

Standard
Presented to the Legion Condor at the Barajas Parade. It bears the streamer of the *Medalla Militar Colectiva* award.

Once the war was over, the German combatants of the Legion Condor took part in a large number of celebratory acts organized by various towns and cities in recognition of their part in the victory of the Nationalist forces, but the two most important events were the air tattoo at Barajas on May 12 and the Victory Parade through the streets of Madrid a week later.

Parade
An aerial view of the Victory Parade held in Madrid in May 1939. Group F/88 of the Legion Condor can be seen in the photo.

Presidential box
Franco, accompanied by von Richthofen, viewing the passage of a 20mm anti-aircraft battery at the Madrid Victory Parade.

DESFILE DE LA VICTORIA

MADRID - 19 de Mayo de 1939

In the former, between 4,500 and 5,000 German volunteers, practically all from ground units (anti-aircraft artillery, communications technicians, mechanics, drivers), paraded together with their Spanish and Italian comrades-in-arms. During the proceedings a number of commanders, officers and NCOs of the Legion Condor were awarded the *Medalla Militar* (Military Medal) by Franco, who also presented *General* von Richthofen with colors for the Unit.

One week after this splendid parade, May 19 to be precise, Madrid was witness to the most important event of its kind to be held at that time: the Victory Parade through the streets of the capital. This grand parade, which

Autograph
Above, left. A captain of the Legion Condor signs an autograph for three young women from Leon.

Podium
Above, right. Authorities of Leon preside over the parade of the Legion Condor from this vantage point.

Arch
One of the many arches adorning Leon during the days when the city was bidding the Legion Condor farewell.

Notes on the German Intervention

Farewell
Center, left. Stamped invitation to the military parade of the Legion Condor at the La Virgen del Camino airfield (Leon).

Streets of Leon
A large number of commemorative arches were set up in many streets of the city of Leon, as can be seen in the photos on this page.

lasted all of six hours, included representatives of the German volunteers who marched with the official colors – recently presented on May 12 at Barajas – to the fore.

The time had come to repatriate the members of the Legion Condor remaining in Spain and tribute was paid to them in an official send-off in deserved recognition of a job well done. The farewell parade, presided over by *Generalísimo* Franco, took place on May 22, 1939 close to the city of Leon, at the airfield of La Virgen del Camino, which had been one of the most important airfields used by the German air force units throughout the war.

LEGION CONDOR

After receiving their accolade the German combatants were assembled at Vigo from where on May 26 they would set sail for Germany on board five vessels belonging to *"Kraft durch Freude"* (Strength through Joy), a section of the German Labor Front. So ended the successful cooperation of the German militia with Spain's Nationalist forces.

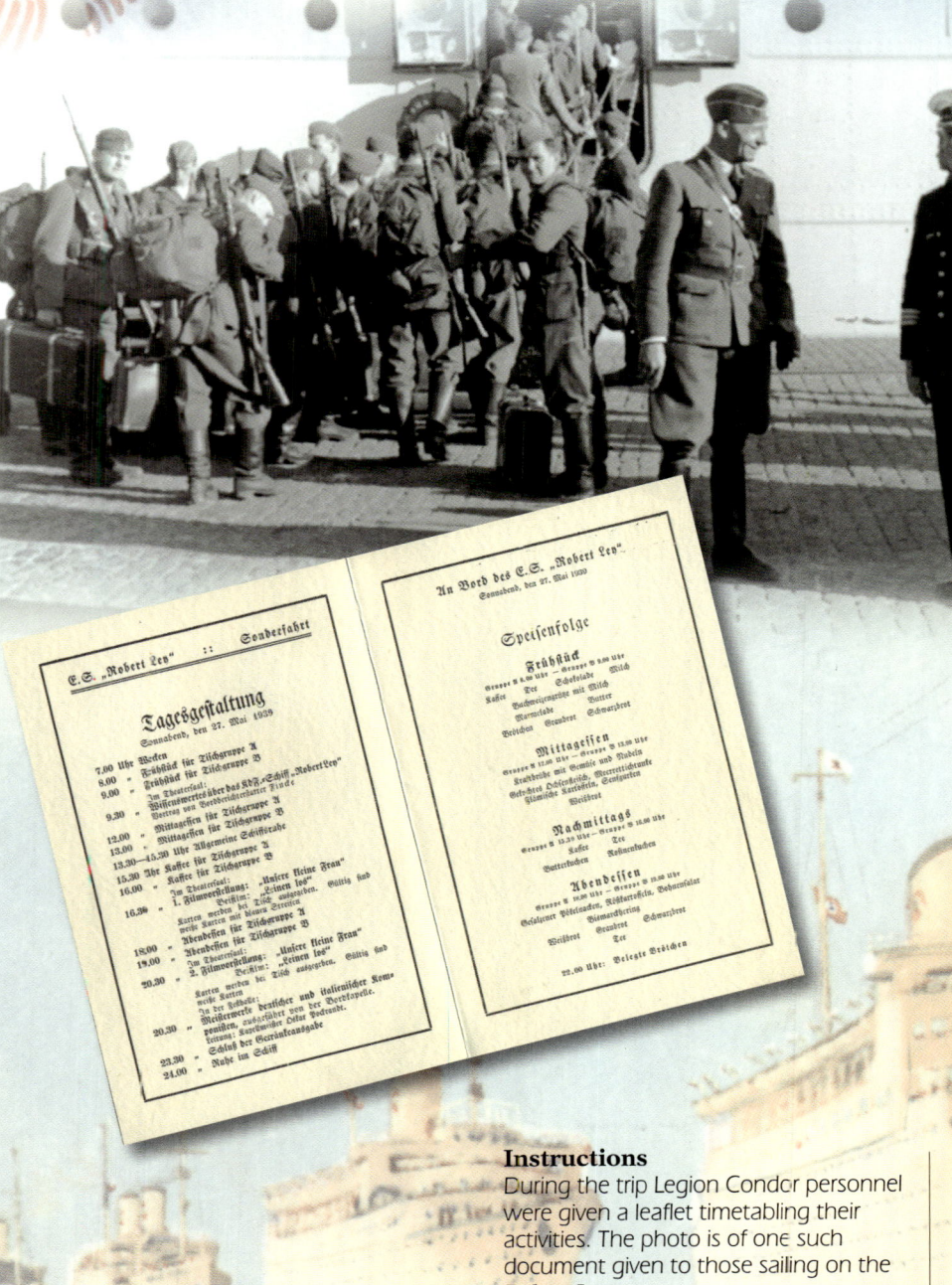

Going aboard
German troops, with combat gear and suitcases, board ship to return to Germany.

Instructions
During the trip Legion Condor personnel were given a leaflet timetabling their activities. The photo is of one such document given to those sailing on the *Robert Ley*.

Fishing boat
Above. Citizens of Vigo on board a trawler decked out for the occasion bid farewell to the German vessels.

Vigo
Below. This Galician trading and fishing port was the point of departure for the ex-combatants of the Legion Condor.

Back home they were feted and welcomed as heroes returning from taking part in the struggle against communism in a distant, and for many of their countrymen, practically unknown land.

Farewell
Legion Condor soldiers on deck aboard the steamships that would take them home.

Ensign
Below. The German vessels raised the official ensign of the Legion Condor during the return trip to Germany.

Notes on the German Intervention

Spanish Cross
Right. German medal awarded at different grades to members of the Legion Condor. In the photo, the Spanish Cross in Silver with Swords.

Mast
The Legion Condor's flag flies from the main mast of one of the vessels.

Kraft durch Freude
Below. The official German organization "Strength through Joy," chartered the vessels used to repatriate the Legion Condor. In the photo, the *Wilhelm Gustloff*.

Legion Condor

Reception
Several photos showing the official reception given to the Legion Condor in Hamburg. These acts were presided over by the then Air Minister, Marshall Hermann Göring, who reviewed the troops and watched the parade. At his side, at all times, was the recently arrived commander of the contingent, General Wolfram von Richthofen, who was wearing a number of Spanish medals and insignia.

Legion Condor

Medals
Left. Military Merit Crosses with red and white distinctive (respectively), and Campaign Medal. The manner of wearing the medals was typical of the German army.

Parade
Right and below. Military parade through the streets of Hamburg. The photos reflect the festive atmosphere that reigned during the parade.

Music
In Hamburg the band of the Legion Condor also paraded.

Foreign militia
Below. Foreign guests together with various members of the Legion Condor.

Berlin
Great military parade in Berlin. This was the final event of the celebrations organized in Germany to honor the victorious return of the unit of German volunteers who fought in the Spanish Civil War. It was presided over by Führer and Reich Chancellor Adolf Hitler.

CHAPTER II

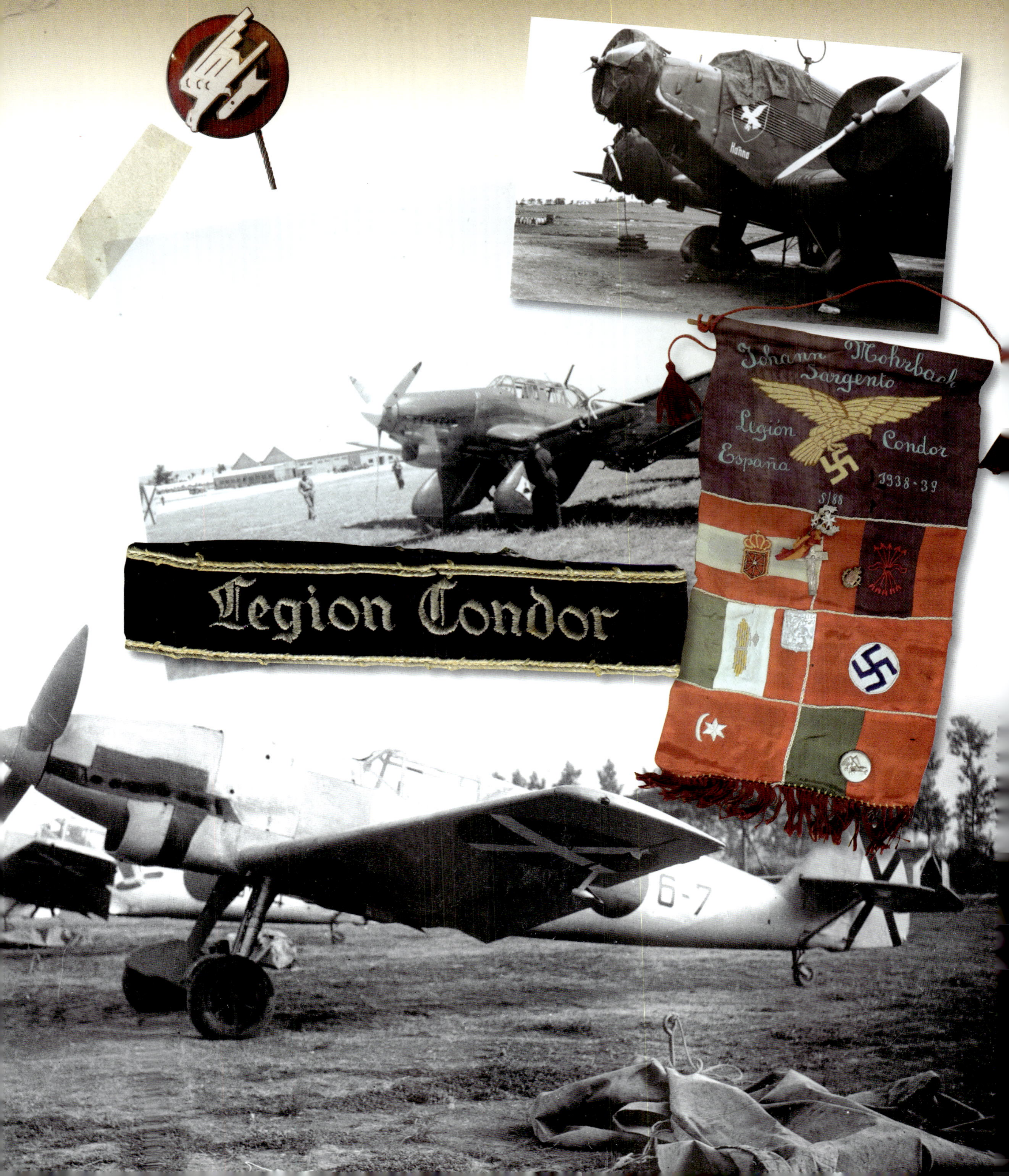

Hanna
Johann Mohrbach
Sargento
Legión
Condor
España
1938-39
S/88
Legion Condor
6-7

The Role Played by the Air Force

Badge
Non-regulation handmade badge to which a swastika has been added.

Twin-engined aircraft
Gradually Germany started sending to Spain the most advanced aircraft it had, for example, the twin-engined Heinkel He 111.

The Legion Condor had a complex organization. Germany sent to Spain not only air force units but also ground and naval forces which played a very important role, on the one hand in the training of Spanish command cadres, and on the other in direct involvement in combat with units of tanks, field artillery, etc.

However, the bulk of the Legion Condor was made up of a sizable collection of air force units, equipped with aircraft covering all operational needs. So in Spain there were groups and squadrons of bombers, fighters, tactical and strategic reconnaissance, seaplanes, as well as experimental units composed of aircraft that were being tested for the first time under operational conditions in Spain. The Legion also had other aviation-related components, such as anti-aircraft artillery, signals units and other logistical and support units, such as assembly and repair depots, munitions units, medical units, etc.

In this chapter we take a detailed look at the flying units, before dealing one by one with the other units we have mentioned.

S/88
The Legion Condor's command unit comprised both civilian and military staff.

1. *Führungsstab*, S/88. High Command, General Staff and associated services

Eagle
Center. Official badge identifying members of the recently formed Luftwaffe.

Sperrle
Below. The first commander of the German expeditionary force was General Hugo Sperrle.

The General Staff of the Legion Condor, under the direct control of the commander-in-chief, was a more streamlined organization than usual, being basically formed by two Sections, Section I (with three subsections, referred to as Ia (command), Ib (operations) and Ic (information)) and Section II (also known as the *Quartiermeister*), responsible for the logistics services required to ensure the operational readiness of the unit.

The first commander of the Legion Condor, Hugo Sperrle (codename Sander), arrived in Spain together with his General Staff, aboard a Junkers Ju 52 that flew from Rome to Melilla towards the end of November 1936.

Operations in the north
General Sperrle personally oversaw a number of operations carried out on the Northern front.

After a short stay in Seville, the S/88 was stationed in Salamanca, near the *Generalísimo*'s first headquarters. From this base the leader of the Legion Condor directed the operations flown by its air force units, over the Madrid front, the Northern front, the Andalusian front and at the battles of Jarama and Guadalajara.

Silver table
Below. When Hugo Sperrle left Spain, his subordinates made him a gift of this table, made by melting down and recasting 328 Spanish silver coins, on which was engraved the most important places he had passed through.

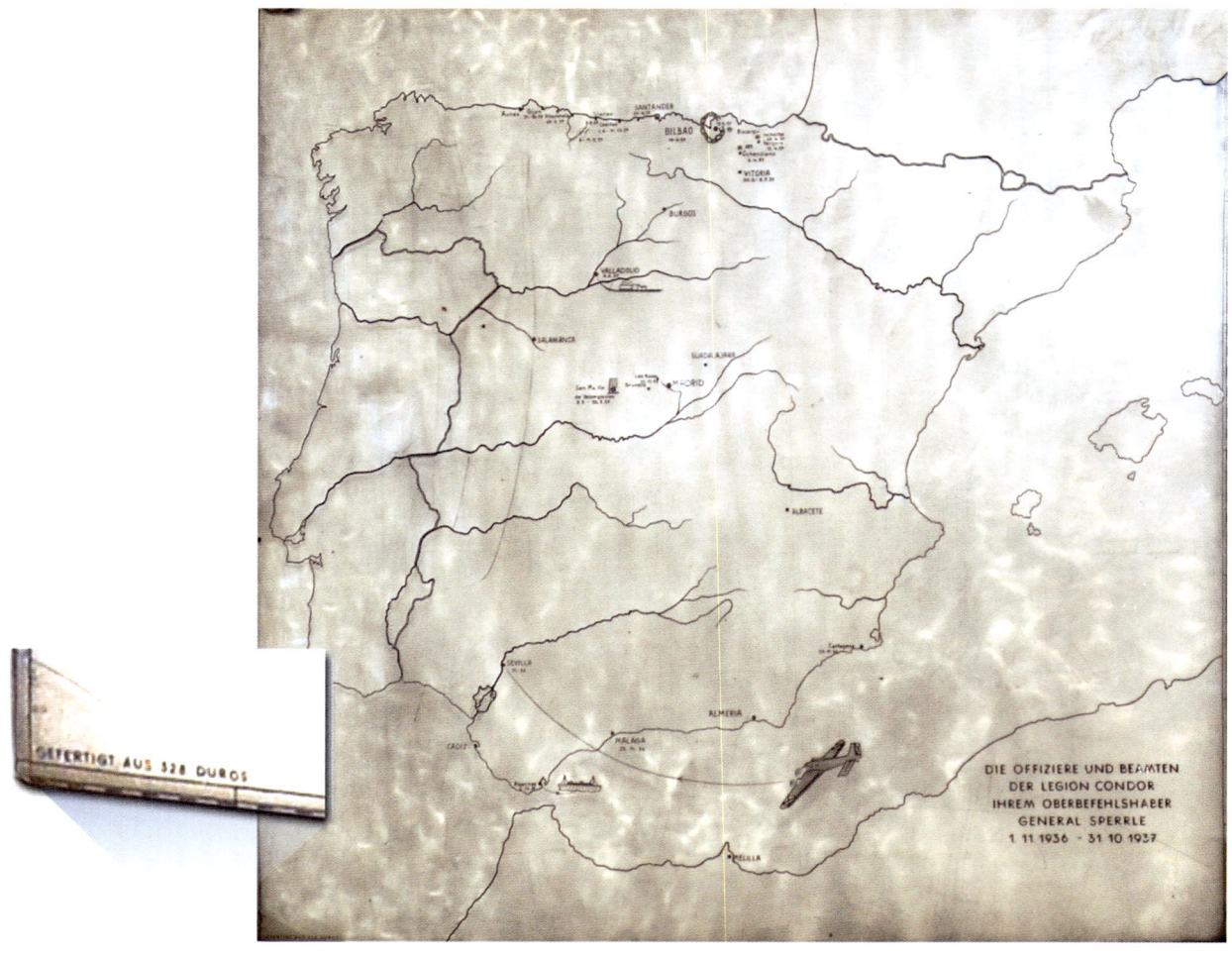

Document
Above, Left. Certificate of the award of the Spanish Cross in silver without swords to an interpreter of S/88.

Cigarette case
Center. Damascened cigarette case, made in Toledo for members of the Legion Condor.

Personnel
Above, right. Two officers of the Headquarters of the Legion Condor.

Early in 1937 *Oberstleutnant* Von Richthofen relieved Alexander Holle from his post as Chief of General Staff, and late in March 1937, with the Basque front resolved, *Stab/88* headquarters was moved from Salamanca to Vitoria (Álava). Von Richthofen was given command of all the air force units to be involved in the planned offensive against the Basque Country, including the Italian and Spanish air forces assigned to the Northern front.

Thanks to Von Richthofen's diary we know the names of some of the members of his General Staff, both German and Spanish. So we know that the Spanish officer responsible for liaising with the Legion Condor was the *Capitán de Corbeta*, naval observer and aeronautical engineer, Manuel de la Sierra Bustamante.

Visit
Above. Franco visiting the headquarters of the Legion Condor. At left is Oberst Plocher chief of staff of the German forces.

Fieseler Storch
Left. These aircraft served S/88 in both liaison and reconnaissance roles.

Air Commander
Above and center, right. *General* Alfredo Kindelán visited the German headquarters at La Cenia. In the photos he is seen with *Generalleutnant* Volkmann and his interpreter, *Major* Max Buch.

Staff car
Staff car of the commander of the Legion Condor.

Accommodation
Members of S/88 relax in their billets in Almazán (Soria). On the right, *Generalleutnant* Volkmann.

With regard to the German staff, Richthofen mentions Spindler, information officer, *Hauptmann* Meier, translator of orders, *Oberleutnant* Hans Asmus of Section Ia (Command), *Oberleutnant* Heinz Runze, Asmus's successor, *Hauptmann* Trettner, of Section II (*Quartiermeister*), and liaison officers with Spanish ground units, such as *Hauptmann* Hansemann, for the 4th Brigade of Navarre. He also mentions an officer called Lieb, who we have not been able to identify.

After a brief visit to the Madrid front, where Sperrle led his air force units in the Battle of Brunete, Stab/88 returned to the North at the end of July 1937 to take part in the offensive against Santander and later against

THE ROLE PLAYED BY THE AIR FORCE

Asturias. After capturing the Cantabrian capital, the General Staff of the Legion Condor moved to that city and remained there until the end of the Asturian campaign in late October 1937. The Legion Condor sent its materiel to be serviced at the Leon depot and the air unit remained inactive for practically the whole of November, although by the end of the month they were in a state of readiness for the big Madrid offensive.

By December 1937 the S/88 had set up their base in the village of Almazán, in the province the Soria, and was taken by surprise there by the attack of Popular Republican Army on Teruel. By then *Generalleutnant* Hellmuth Volkmann had taken command of the Legion Condor, aided by a new Chief of General Staff, Herman Plocher.

Enamel ornament
Above. Ornament representing the friendship between the countries supporting the Nationalist cause.

Klemm
Center. Klemm Kl 32 light aircraft used for liaison duties.

Almazán
Above, right. Full complement of S/88 top brass attending a meeting at Almazán.

Visit from Franco
Lined up in front of a Fieseler Storch, members of S/88 and the Generalísimo's Staff during the visit the latter paid to La Cenia airfield.

Legion Condor

Franco and Volkmann
The commander of the Legion Condor, Hellmuth Volkmann chats with the *Generalísimo* Franco while smoking a cigarette.

After the Republican zone had been split in two, Stab/88 moved to San Mateo, a small town close to Vinaroz (Castellón), and shortly after to Benicarló, a little further south. From there Volkmann commanded his units stationed at the airfields of La Cenia, Alfaro and Buñuel during the Valencia offensive.

Command
Generalleutnant Volkmann took over command of the Legion Condor from Hugo Sperrle in November of 1937.

Navarre Brigades
Center. The Legion Condor provided direct support to the Navarre Army Corps in a number of operations. In the photo, a cloth badge of those units.

Vehicles
The S/88 used a number of different vehicles for staff transport duties.

The Role Played by the Air Force

These operations against Valencia were frustrated by the surprise crossing of the Ebro by the Republican army on July 25, 1938, after which the Legion Condor's General Staff moved its headquarters to Baños de Fitero (Logroño).

Once the Battle of the Ebro was over, at the end of November 1938, there was a change in the command of the Legion Condor and the post was given to *Generalmajor* Wolfram Von Richtofen, accompanied by his Chief of General Staff, *Oberstleutnant* Hans Seidemann. This team was responsible for directing the operations of the German air force unit against Catalonia and, once the French border had been reached, for preparing the final offensive in the center of Spain, in March 1939. The two commanders were also responsible for organizing the repatriation of the Legion Condor, in May 1939.

To close this section we should mention that a number of single-engined aircraft were attached to *Stab/88* for liaison and air-taxi duties: Junkers W 34 hi, Klemm Kl 32 a XIV, Messerschmitt Bf 108 B, and Fiseler Fi 156 A.

Dagger
Above, right. Members of the Legion Condor acquired a number of souvenirs made of the damascened steel Toledo is famous for.

Staff
Above, left. Hermann Plocher, Chief of Staff of the Legion Condor, with Volkmann.

Badge
Center. Metal pilot's badge and air observer.

Flag
At some of the military facilities of the Legion Condor, the official flag of the Third Reich flew, as can be seen in the photo.

Legion Condor

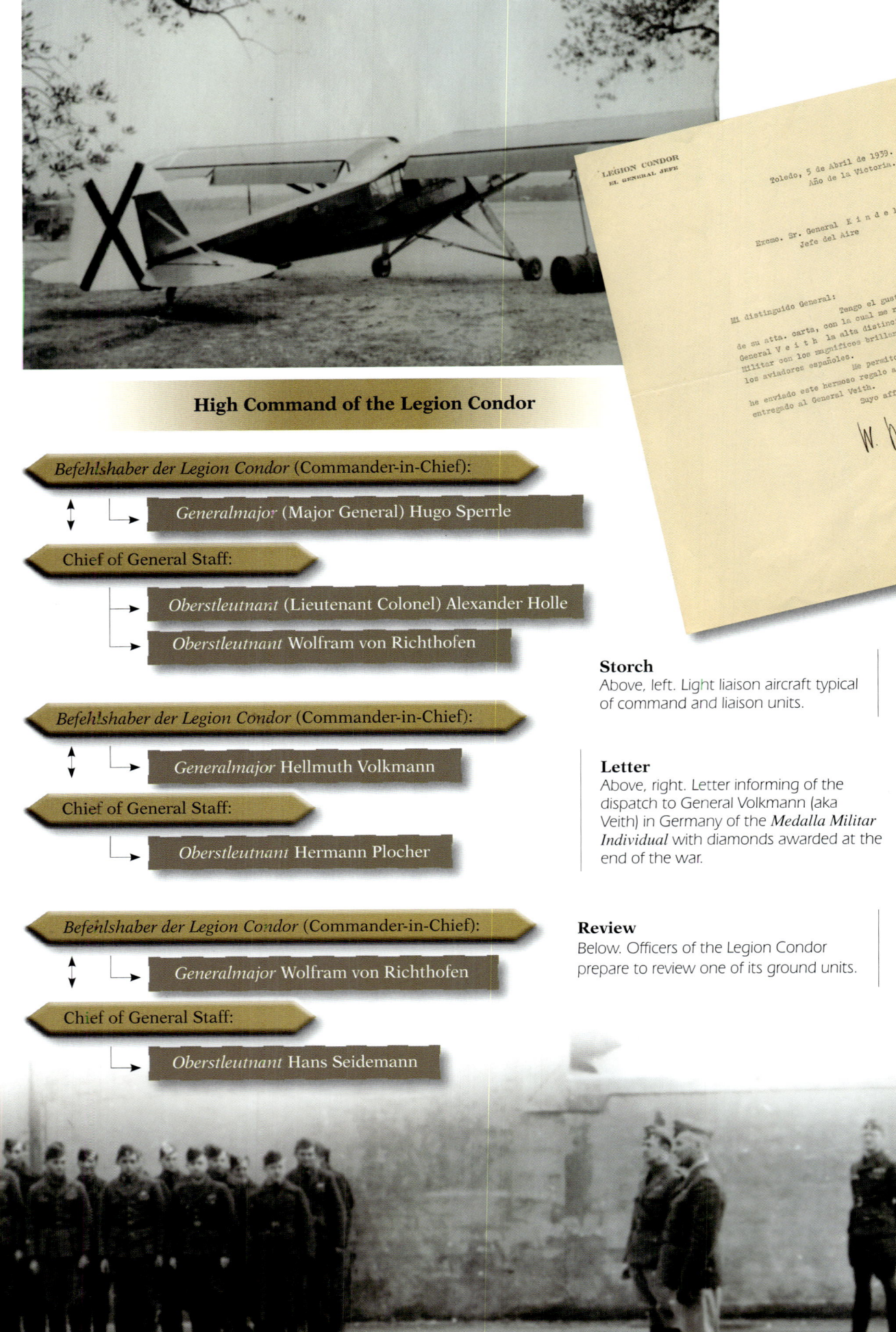

High Command of the Legion Condor

Befehlshaber der Legion Condor (Commander-in-Chief):
→ *Generalmajor* (Major General) Hugo Sperrle

Chief of General Staff:
→ *Oberstleutnant* (Lieutenant Colonel) Alexander Holle
→ *Oberstleutnant* Wolfram von Richthofen

Befehlshaber der Legion Condor (Commander-in-Chief):
→ *Generalmajor* Hellmuth Volkmann

Chief of General Staff:
→ *Oberstleutnant* Hermann Plocher

Befehlshaber der Legion Condor (Commander-in-Chief):
→ *Generalmajor* Wolfram von Richthofen

Chief of General Staff:
→ *Oberstleutnant* Hans Seidemann

Storch
Above, left. Light liaison aircraft typical of command and liaison units.

Letter
Above, right. Letter informing of the dispatch to General Volkmann (aka Veith) in Germany of the *Medalla Militar Individual* with diamonds awarded at the end of the war.

Review
Below. Officers of the Legion Condor prepare to review one of its ground units.

Generalleutnant Freiherr v. Richthofen

THE ROLE PLAYED BY THE AIR FORCE

Heinkel 51
Above. Standard fighter of the Luftwaffe in 1936.

Letter opener
Center. This belonged to a member of Group J/88.

La Cenia
Center. He 51 biplanes camouflaged among the trees.

2.*Jagdgruppe*, J-88. Fighter Group

When the Legion Condor was officially formed early in November 1936, it included a fighter group made up of three newly formed squadrons and a fourth comprising the surviving aircraft from those sent from Germany in the previous months which had already been fighting in the skies over Spain since mid August.

In the first months all these units were equipped with Heinkel He 51 biplanes which, apart from those already in Spain, of course, arrived at Cadiz on November 18, suitably disguised as farm machinery.

"Marabú"
Insigni used by the Heinkel He 51s of 1.J/88.

Fourth Squadron
Squadron 4.J/88 has the ace of spades as its emblem.

Legion Condor

The first commander of the Group was *Major* Hubertus von Merhardt and the various squadrons were led by *Hauptmann* Werner Palm, and *Oberleutnants* Otto Lehmann, Jürgen Roth and Herwin Knüppel (the latter replaced *Oberleutnant* Kraft Eberhardt who was killed in action on November 13 of that same year).

Around this time, dogfights with enemy fighters, which by late 1936 were mostly Polikarpov I-15s and I-16s, which were clearly superior to the He 51s, were a regular occurrence over all the active fronts and in the skies over Madrid, the outcome of which was a great many victories, but also the loss of a number of aircraft and also pilots. The morale of the German pilots suffered as a result of flying inferior aircraft and they had to call on their personal flying skills and bravery to redress the balance.

Mickey Mouse
The Heinkel He 51s of Squadron 3.J/88 bore a Mickey Mouse emblem.

Dog tags
Center. ID tags of German pilots in Spain.

German fighter
After a time painted gray, the He 51s received a new livery.

The Role Played by the Air Force

Adolf Galland's aircraft
This He 51 coded 2•78 was the personal airplane of *Oberleutnant* Adolf Galland, 3.J/88 squadron leader. In addition to bearing the "Mickey Mouse" emblem, the aircraft also had a *Tatzenkreuz* (cross patty) in white on the typical black circle of the Nationalist air force (the circle also edged in white), which was the personal emblem of that officer in Spain.

In March 1937, the 2nd Squadron received a new type of aircraft to replace their now obsolete He 51s: the Messerschmitt Bf 109 B.1, a closed cockpit monoplane.

In that same month, the 4th Squadron was disbanded, leaving only three operational. Of these three, the 1st and the 3rd, which were still equipped with biplanes rendered obsolete for fighter missions, were assigned to tactical support duties, a role in which they proved to be highly effective.

Early in August 1937, after taking part in the Battle of Brunete, the 1st squadron also switched to Messerschmitt Bf 109s, but in their case it was B.2 version, which was fitted with a variable-pitch metal propeller, unlike the B.1 version that had wooden blades.

Ground attack
The latest German Heinkel He 51s were used for attacking ground forces.

Legion Condor

He 51s in profile
From above to below:
- Aircraft of 3.J/88, used by Doctor Neumann.
- Aircraft of 4.J/88.
- Aircraft of 3.J/88.

Souvenir
Right. A member of 2.J/88 made this bracelet with silver coins of the day and an enemy projectile that hit on December 28, 1938.

THE ROLE PLAYED BY THE AIR FORCE

Knüppel
Right. Cockpit of the Heinkel He 51 of *Oberleutnant* Erwin Knüppel, commander of the first German fighter unit before the Legion Condor came to Spain. The aircraft has a top hat painted on the side, the same emblem that Squadron 2.J/88 would adopt.

Calparsoro
The Spanish pilot José Ramón Calparsoro photographed in front of a German He 51. Later this pilot would fly with the K/88.

Emblems
From left to right and from top to bottom:
- 4.J/88
- 3.J/88
- Aircraft He 51 2•85
- Aircraft He 51 2•102
- 1.J/88
- Personal emblem

German biplane
Right. The Heinkel He 51 soon showed itself to be inferior to its Soviet counterparts.

Early in November, with the Asturias campaign concluded, the 4th Squadron was reformed and the entire Group was assembled at the La Virgen del Camino airfield, near Leon, for their aircraft to be serviced and for their crews to enjoy some well-deserved leave.

The next great military confrontation in which the aircraft of J/88 took part was the Battle of Teruel. In this fierce battle the He 51s of the 3rd Squadron kept up a relentless attack on the enemy troops whenever

6•75
Above. *Teniente* Goy, just back from a mission, waves to the camera.

Maintenance
Mechanics inspect the engine of a Bf 109.

Mickey Mouse
Metal Mickey Mouse badge.

THE ROLE PLAYED BY THE AIR FORCE

Emblems
- 6•75, *Teniente* Goy.
- 6•51, *Hauptmann* Schellmann
- 6•10, unknown pilot

Captured
Previous page, below and profile. This aircraft, piloted by *Unteroffizier* Otto Polenz, fell into Republican hands, undamaged, in December 1937. It belonged to 1.J/88.

the extreme weather conditions allowed, from a few days after the Republican army started its operations in mid-December 1937 until the Nationalist forces brought the engagement to a successful conclusion in February 1938. The unit lost three aircraft between December 1937 and the end of February 1938. Meanwhile, the two squadrons equipped with Me 109s had shot down thirty-five Republican aircraft.

Once this battle was over, the Nationalist Army intended to advance through Aragon towards the Mediterranean and so cut the area controlled by the Government of Valencia in two. On this occasion the He 51s and Me 109s once again fulfilled the objectives set for them by high command, albeit at a cost. They suffered a number of casualties; three pilots were killed and one was taken prisoner).

Twin blade
The first Messerschmitts proved to be greatly superior to enemy fighters.

La Cenia
Left. A twin-bladed Bf 109 at La Cenia airfield.

Millán Astray
Right. *General* José Millán Astray, founder of *La Legión*, chats with Handrick, commander of Group J/88 of the Legion Concor.

The 4th squadron was disbanded once again in mid-June 1938 and the following month the He 51s of the 3rd Squadron were replaced by Bf 109 Ds, so that now all three of the Group's squadrons were equipped with monoplanes (109s types B, C and D).

The entire unit took part in the Battle of the Ebro, fought from July until November 1938. The latest versions of the Bf 109 received, the C and D types, were significantly superior to the most modern enemy fighters, the Polikarpov I-16s, so the skies were now permanently ruled by the German monoplanes. The squadrons were to suffer no fatalities in action.

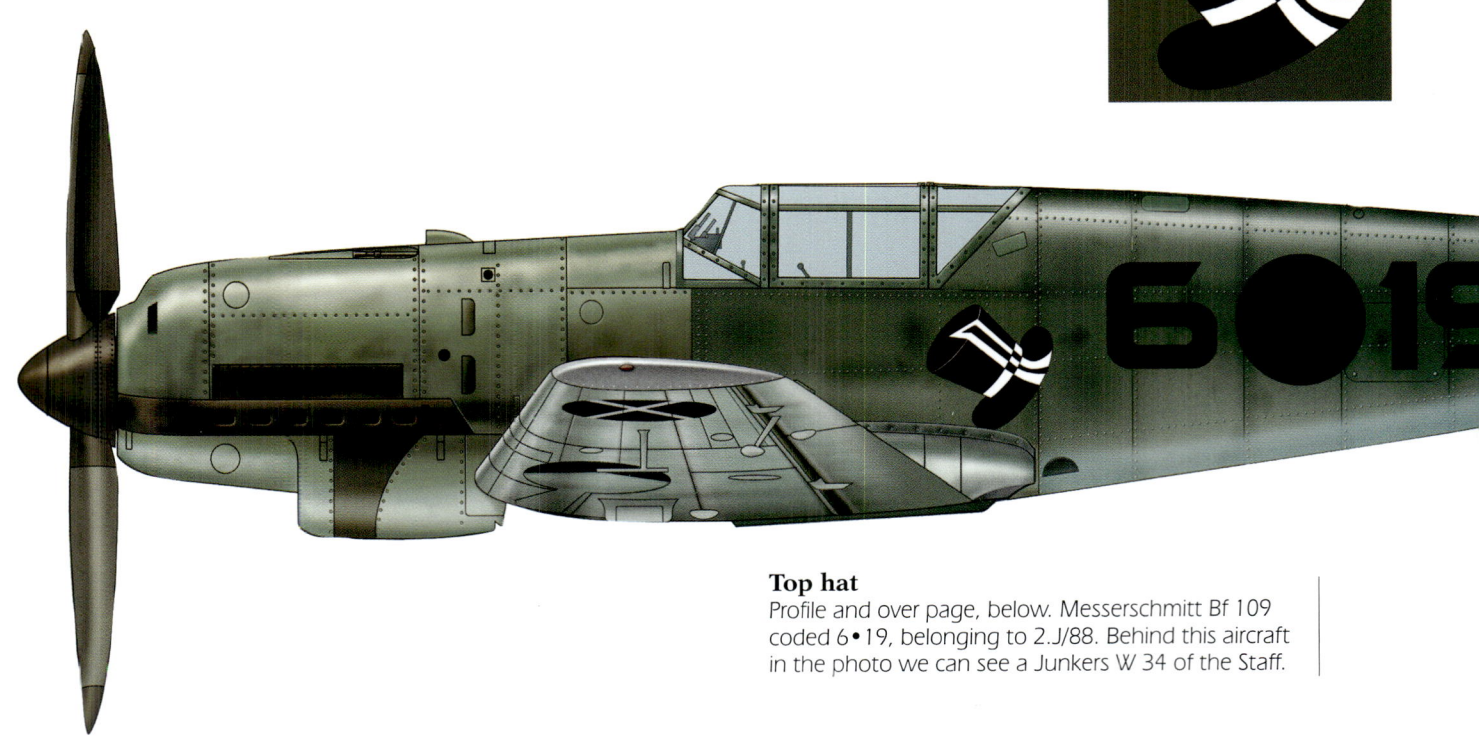

Top hat
Profile and over page, below. Messerschmitt Bf 109 coded 6•19, belonging to 2.J/88. Behind this aircraft in the photo we can see a Junkers W 34 of the Staff.

THE ROLE PLAYED BY THE AIR FORCE

Personal emblem
Above, left. Olympic rings and the letter "H" on the Bf 109 6•56 of Group J/88 leader, Gotthardt Handrick.

Mölders
Above, right. The Bf 109 6•79, nicknamed *Luchs* (Lynx), was the aircraft used by *Hauptmann* Werner Mölders, the Legion Condor's top ace.

The Germans fighters played a similarly outstanding role during the Catalonian campaign, now with the three squadrons mostly re-equipped with Bf 109s of the new E.1 and E.3 versions (although they still kept some aircraft of the previous series). As the Nationalist Army advanced towards the French border, the fighters occupied the airfields that the enemy were abandoning, and so were able to cooperate more closely with the ground troops.

Legion Condor

Miscellaneous
Various objects, medals and photos belonging to airmen serving in the Legion Condor.

THE ROLE PLAYED BY THE AIR FORCE

During these operations one event stands out as particularly memorable: the attack in the early hours of February 6, 1939 by monoplanes of the 1st Squadron on the airfield at Vilajuiga, Gerona. The raid ended with twenty-seven enemy aircraft of various types destroyed on the ground. From that moment until the end of the Catalonian campaign, the German fighters were scarcely troubled by what was left of the enemy fighter squadrons and were able to increase

Accident
This Bf 109B suffered serious damage after a crash landing.

La Cenia
Below and over page, below. Fighters of J/88 are camouflaged among the trees round the airfield.

The Role Played by the Air Force

Bf 109 6•79
Hauptmann Mölders talking to ground staff responsible for maintaining his aircraft.

Bf 109E
Aircraft 6•111, belonging to 2.J/88. Note that it has a three-bladed propeller, unlike the series B, C and D.

Air victories
Hauptmann Mölders' Bf 109D-1 has twelve white bars painted on the tail, one for each of his victories up until then. It also displays the Mickey Mouse emblem of 3.J/88.

their tally of victories without loss.

In the two months or less that remained of the war, the Legion Condor's Fighter Group flew few missions and its various units transferred to their new home at the Barcience-Torrijos airfield in the province of Toledo in preparation for the final offensive of the war. The last mission to be flown involved a number of Bf 109s that were assigned to provide and escort to some twin-engined He 111s

6•100
Center. An E series Messerschmitt at La Cenia airfield.

Machine gun
Left. One of the MG 17 machine guns the Messerschmitt was armed with.

The Role Played by the Air Force

Three-bladed
Right. A Bf 109E-3 fitted with 20mm MG FF cannons on the wings.

of K/88 on a bombing raid against enemy positions. The date was March 27, 1939.

To sum up, a total of ninety-three He 51s were sent to Spain in the course of the war and 139 examples of the other model used by the Fighter Group, the Bf 109 in its various versions, also populated the skies of Spain.

Group J/88 shot down a total of 314 enemy aircraft and suffered thirty-four fatal casualties (killed in action, accidents or illness).

Holzauge
Below and center. Aircraft belonging to 1.J/88 with the new emblem adopted after *Hauptmann* Siebelt Reents took command in 1939. This emblem represented a *Holzauge* (Wooden Eye).

The Role Played by the Air Force

Experimental aircraft
The first Henschel Hs 123 to arrive in Spain bore a strange coding and were nicknamed "Angelito" and numbered 1 and 2. In the pictures on the previous page we can see that model, and also the Heinkel 112 and Bf 109 fighter prototypes, which flew in the squadron known as VJ/88.

Swastika
The Heinkel 112 V9 prototype coded 8•2 had a swastika painted inside the black circle, the personal emblem of the *Hauptmann* Harro Harder.

3. *Versuchsjagdstaffel*, VJ/88. The experimental fighter unit

Apart from the fighter aircraft sent to Spain to equip the Legion Condor, the *Luftwaffe* also sent a few aircraft of different models, some prototypes, to be tested under combat conditions.

In October 1936 various such aircraft arrived at Seville: one Heinkel 50G and two Henschel 123, and a little later, three Messerschmitt Bf 109 prototypes (coded V.3, V.4 and V.5), and one Heinkel He 112 fighter. In December a Junkers Ju 87 arrived but shortly after the He 50 and at least one of the Hs 123s were sent back to Germany.

All these aircraft plus three Henschel 123s were grouped in a unit called the Experimental Fighter Squadron (Versuchsjagdstaffel VJ/88). As was also the case with VB/88, a group of civilian specialists originally formed part of this squadron, although as the weeks went by this civilian contingent dwindled in numbers significantly.

The operational life of this unit was relatively short, since at the end of March it was disbanded and its aircraft were absorbed into other units of J/88, except for the Henschel 123s which were used to form a small unit called "*Stuka Kette 88.*"

THE ROLE PLAYED BY THE AIR FORCE

Rayo
The Heinkel He 70, known in Spain as "Rayo" (Lightning), was the most modern aircraft supplied to the Legion Condor when it was first formed.

Accident
Center. Aircraft 14•35, after making a crash landing in which the undercarriage collapsed.

Original livery
The first He 70s of A/88 were painted in the same livery in Spain as in Germany. Note the white lightning bolt on the black background.

4. *AUFKLÄRUNGSSTAFFEL*, A/88. RECONNAISSANCE SQUADRON

One of the German air force units whose missions were of paramount importance, although its vital impact on military operations in the Spanish civil war has gone largely unrecognized, is the group known as A/88.

Its first aircraft, Heinkel He 70 monoplanes (the F photo-reconnaissance and the E light bomber versions), under the orders of *Hauptmann* Heinz Heinsius, were stationed at Avila airfield as part of the initial deployment of Legion Condor air force units, although others were also used depending on the missions assigned over the various fronts.

In flight
A pair of Heinkel He 70s flying over a typical landscape of Spain's central tableland.

Camouflage
Center. After arriving, the He 70s were painted in camouflage colors.

Heinkel He 45
The tactical reconnaissance flight of A/88 used He 45 biplanes.

Towards the middle of November 1936, aircraft of the squadron performed reconnaissance duties over the Madrid front. The He 70s were very fast, giving them a decisive advantage over the Republican fighters that at that time were much slower.

From the end of that month until early May 1937, several He 70s based at Tablada (Seville) flew a number of reconnaissance sorties over the Santa María de la Cabeza monastery in the province of Jaén, within whose walls some troops under the command of *Capitán* Cortés were resisting a siege set by the Republicans. After observing the cessation of all resistance during a flight on May 2 the reconnaissance mission was called off.

In addition to these actions, aircraft A/88 flew several sorties over the Central front (during the battles of the La Coruña Road and Jarama) in the early months of 1937. These sorties were of vital importance as they provided valuable information about the enemy rearguard, as well as bombing strategic targets behind the lines.

The Role Played by the Air Force

Strange decoration
Above. The "Rayo" 14•34 initially sported an odd livery: oblique stripes of an undefined color over the original light gray. This aircraft took part in the bombing raids on the electrical power plants in the Pyrenees.

Pennant
Above, right. Many Legionnaires had this type of souvenir made up by the seamstresses of the villages where they were stationed.

Meanwhile, in the middle of February, three He 70s attacked hydroelectric power plants at Seira and Pobla de Segur, both of which were severely damaged and put out of action for over two months. Two days later, it was the turn of the power plants at Cabdella and San Lorenzo, which also suffered damage that kept the former at half output for several months and also reduced the output of the latter for several weeks. All of these power plants were in the Pyrenees and were of major importance to Catalonian industry.

In March 1937 a flight of Heinkel He 45s was added to the unit to fly tactical reconnaissance missions.

After the Nationalist offensive was unleashed on the Northern front, new reconnaissance aircraft were added in the shape of some Dornier Do 17s that had recently arrived from Germany and initially formed part of VB/88 (the Experimental Bomber Squadron). These flew reconnaissance and bombing missions against enemy targets. It was mostly these aircraft that played a major role in the months the campaign lasted, and they suffered several losses of both men and machines.

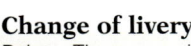

Change of livery
Below. The same aircraft 14•34 would later receive a regulation camouflage paint job.

Biplane
Left. The He 45s were mainly used for artillery spotting missions.

Nose flip
Below. The Heinkel He 45 was prone to this type of accident.

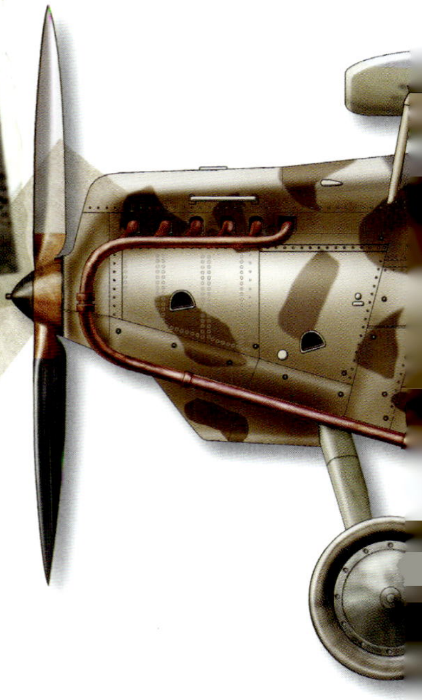

As mentioned earlier, in the middle of the Northern offensive the Battle of Brunete was fought on the Central front. The fast bombers of A/88 were also involved, attacking selected targets and suffering the loss of one Dornier Do 17 and one Heinkel He 70.

The Role Played by the Air Force

Mottled
Above, center (profile) and below, right. The Heinkel He 45 coded 15•6 was painted in unusual camouflage based on irregular blotches reminiscent of the camouflage used by German aircraft during the First World War.

Cufflinks
Made by a renowned jeweler in Madrid at the end of the war, they were engraved with the emblems of the Spanish Nationalist air force, the Italian air force, and the Germar Luftwaffe.

Once the Northern campaign was over, the Legion Condor handed over the remaining He 70s in the Reconnaissance Squadron to the Nationalist Air Force, with the exception of at least two aircraft, which were taken out of front line service and were used instead for mail carrying and liaison duties between German units. Thus at the end of October/beginning of November 1937, A/88 comprised four flights of Do 17 and one of He 45s.

In the autumn of 1937, the Do 17s flew numerous reconnaissance missions over the Aragonese front in preparation for future operations in that sector. And during the hard-fought Battle of Teruel, the twin-engined planes were also involved in a frenzy of activity against the Republican rearguard and other enemy positions.

Legion Condor

Bacalao
Profile and over page, above. While on Germany the Dornier Do 17 was nicknamed the *Flying Pencil*, in Spain they were called *Bacalao* (Cod).

Crewmen
Left. The crew of a Dornier Do 17 normally consisted of three airmen.

In preparation for the start of the major operation planned by the Nationalist Army to advance through the *Maestrazgo* mountain range towards the Mediterranean which was launched in March 1938, the Legion Condor Reconnaissance Squadron carried out a series of photographic sorties over enemy lines. The results of these sorties were closely studied by members of the unit's general staff and used to make maps on which to plot the enemy forces' positions. These missions were of vital importance to the success of the advance.

Pendant
Above, left. Damascened piece with a Legion motif.

Twin-engined Do 17
Below. Views of two twin-engined Do 17s used by the Legion Condor for long-range reconnaissance sorties.

128

Clogs
Previous page, center. Silver souvenir made for a German member of the Legion Condor.

27•7
Below. This aircraft had a lightning bolt painted near the nose with the name of its unit "A/88" above.

With the Aragon and Levante campaigns underway, the Do 17s made countless bombing raids against Republican positions, railways and troop concentrations, suffering the loss of only one aircraft that was hit by the anti-aircraft artillery. The advance progressed at such a lightning pace that it was necessary to push forward the air bases of the aircraft cooperating with the ground forces. As from March 26 He 45s of A/88 were based at the Sariñena airfield. When the Nationalist troops arrived at the Mediterranean and split the Republican zone in two before pushing along the coast towards Valencia, the enemy points of resistance and fortifications were constantly attacked by Group A/88 aircraft which met with an effective anti-aircraft defense which succeeded in damaging some machines.

LEGION CONDOR

Once the Battle of the Ebro broke out, the Nationalist advance on Valencia was brought to a halt and a large number of troops and aircraft were diverted to the new military hotspot. The aircraft of the German Reconnaissance Squadron were extraordinarily active in the sector, flying reconnaissance and bombing missions against Republican positions from their bases at Buñuel (Navarre)

Devil's head
Above. The same aircraft as on the page before. In this photo we can see the devil's head motif, the unit's emblem, painted on one of its engines.

Drinking cup
Left. A crewmember of Do 17 27•10 probably had this silver cup engraved by a Spanish jeweler.

Emblem
Below. The Do 17s coded 27•7 and 27•8 bore different versions of the emblem of the unit on its engines.

THE ROLE PLAYED BY THE AIR FORCE

Medals
Right. Spanish and German medals belonging to a former combatant of the Legion Condor.

Emblem
Center. In the later stages of the war, the Legion Condor received a number of P series aircraft, with radial engines. The one we see in illustration was handed over to the Spanish at the end of the war.

Dornier Do 17 27•3
This aircraft has the pilot's personal emblem painted below the cockpit; a piglet wearing a top hat. Like the other aircraft in its unit, on the engine there is a devil's head motif.

Personal emblem
Left. Below the cockpit of a Do 17 we can see the personal emblem of an unknown pilot of A/88.

Inspection
A lateral ladder was used to get inside a Do 17

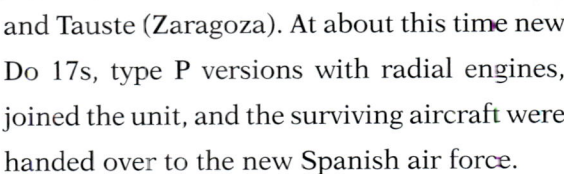

and Tauste (Zaragoza). At about this time new Do 17s, type P versions with radial engines, joined the unit, and the surviving aircraft were handed over to the new Spanish air force.

During the Catalonian campaign the unit received a new type of aircraft, the Henschel Hs 126, which would replace the He 45s which were no longer very operational, although they had nevertheless been remarkably effective in all the missions they had flown during the war up until then.

Superpava
Below. Henschel Hs 126 high wing monoplanes arrived in Spain almost at the end of the war to replace the He 45s of A/88. They were nicknamed *Superpava* (Super Turkey Hen).

The Role Played by the Air Force

Campaign airfield
Above. The Hs 126s flew reconnaissance and light bombing missions. In the foreground we see a German Ju 52 with a civil code.

Souvenir
Above, right. Another engraved silver cup, similar to the one shown earlier.

After the first months of 1939, when Catalonia had been fully incorporated into Nationalist Spain, Group A/88's activity was largely focused on photographic reconnaissance duties over enemy airfields in the central zone until the war ended on April 1.

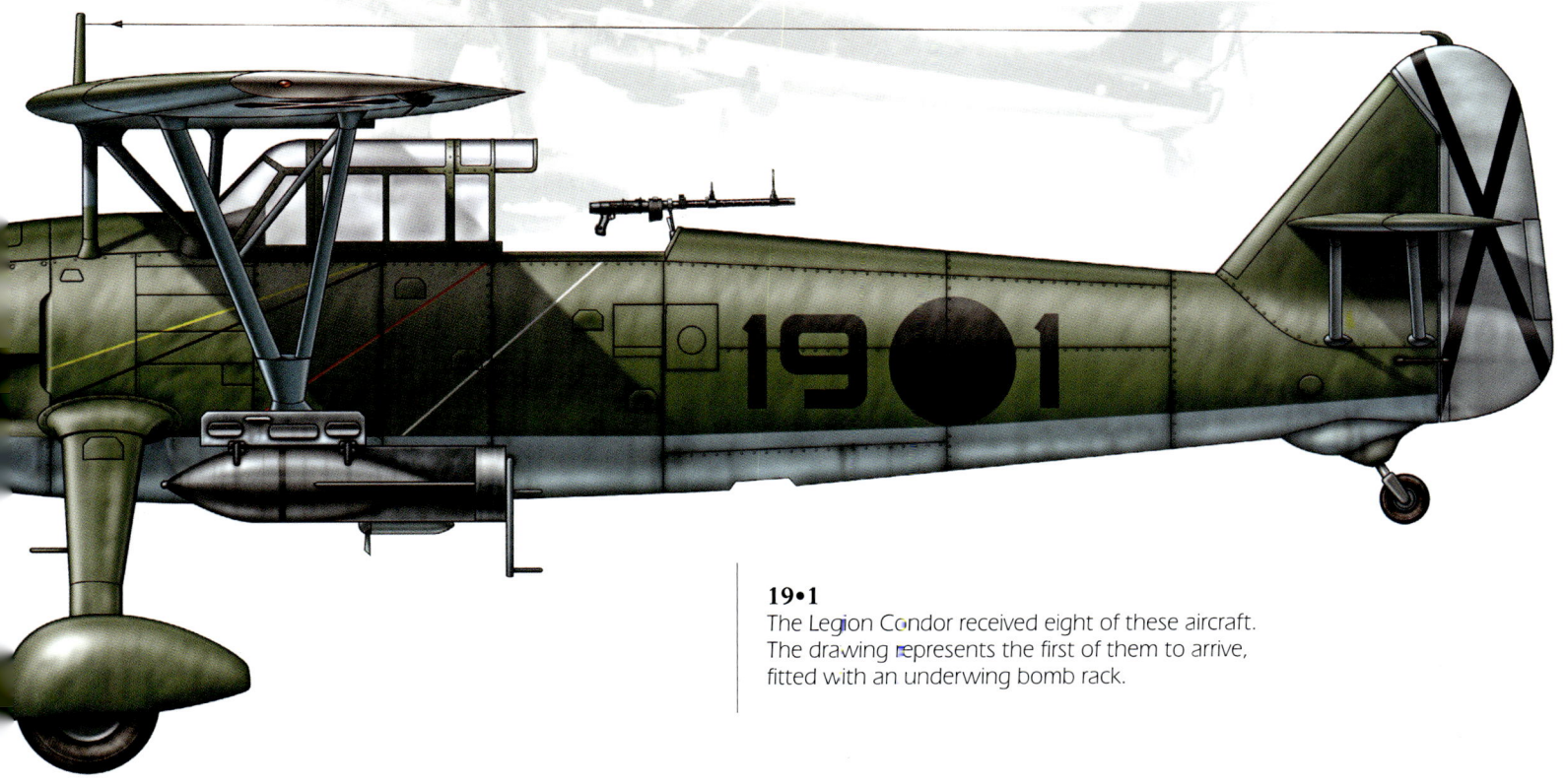

19•1
The Legion Condor received eight of these aircraft. The drawing represents the first of them to arrive, fitted with an underwing bomb rack.

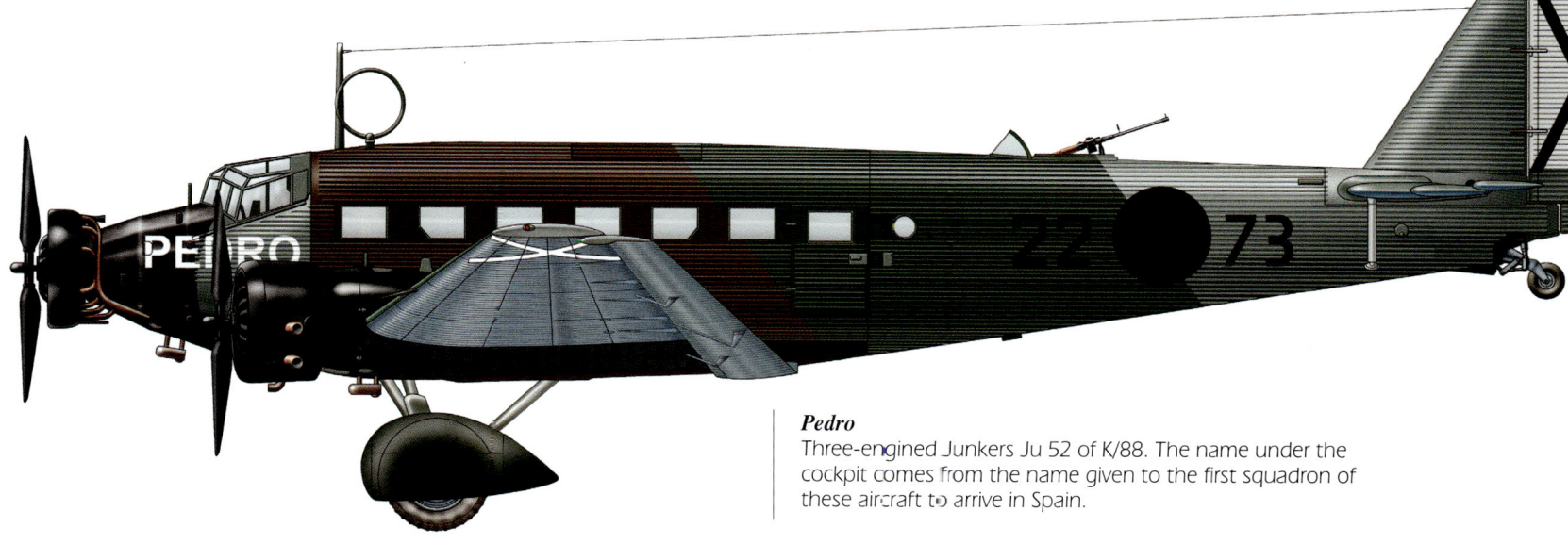

Pedro
Three-engined Junkers Ju 52 of K/88. The name under the cockpit comes from the name given to the first squadron of these aircraft to arrive in Spain.

5. KAMPFGRUPPE, K/88. BOMBER GROUP

The largest air force unit of all Legion Condor units was the Bomber Group, officially called K/88. After the Legion was formed, it was initially composed of three squadrons of twelve three-engined Junkers Ju 52/3mg 3e (nicknamed "*Pablos*" in Spain).

The crews of the first thirty-one bombers to form the *Kampfgruppe* were assembled at Greifswald, Germany, and on November 15, 1936 set off for the Bavarian airfield at Lechfeld, near Augsburg. They took off in small groups from this airfield and flew to the Italian airfield of Ciampino Nord, close to Rome, before flying on to Melilla and then to Seville. By November 19 all the aircraft had arrived and the airfield (Tablada) was to be their base for a short time only, before they were transferred to San Fernando in Salamanca.

Pin
Below, right. This was worn on the lapel of civilian clothing to show that the wearer belonged to that unit, in this case, K/88.

Bombing
Below. The Junkers Ju 52 was designed as a transport aircraft but was converted into an improvised bomber.

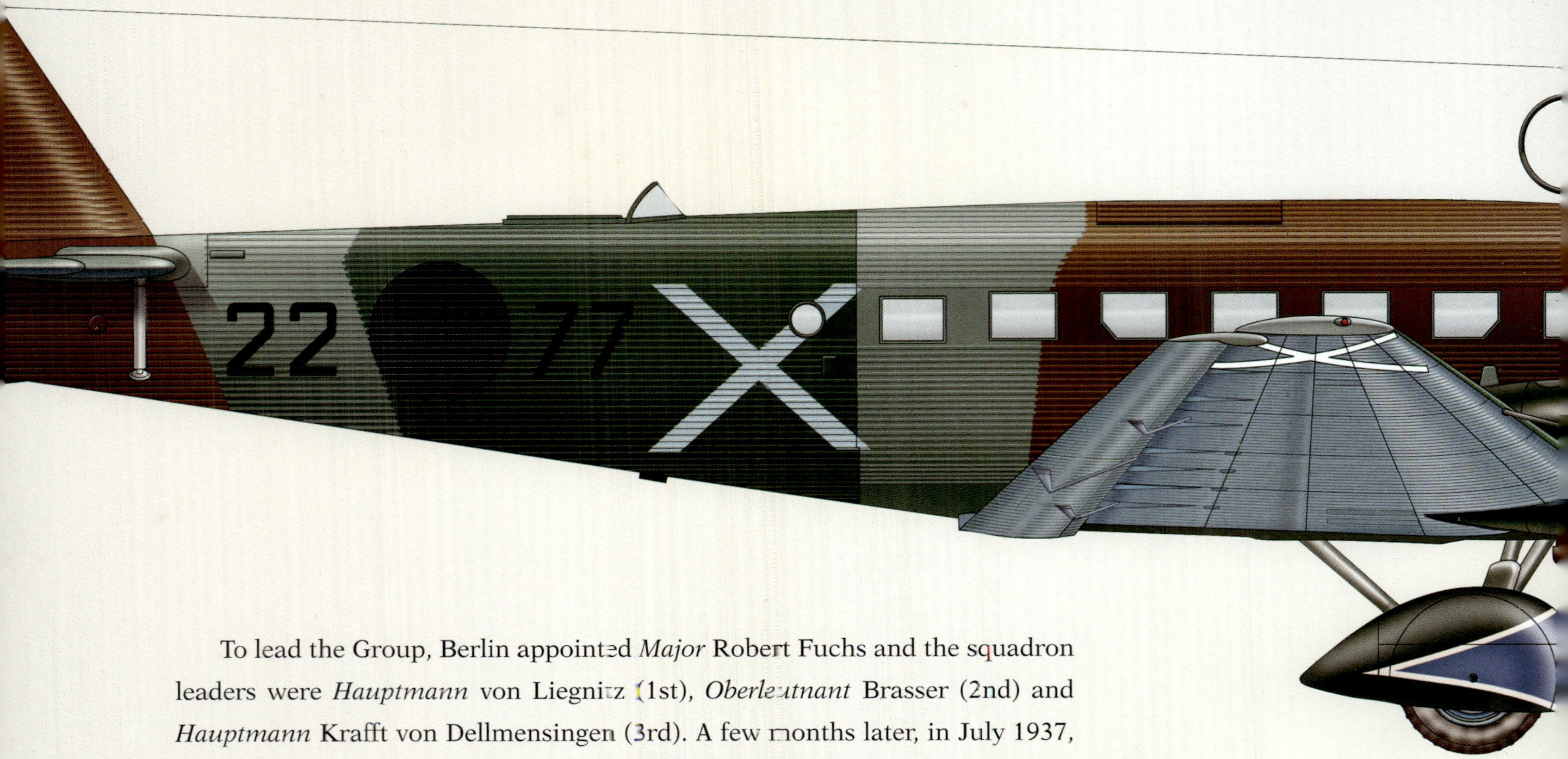

To lead the Group, Berlin appointed *Major* Robert Fuchs and the squadron leaders were *Hauptmann* von Liegnitz (1st), *Oberleutnant* Brasser (2nd) and *Hauptmann* Krafft von Dellmensingen (3rd). A few months later, in July 1937, the *Versuchsbomberstaffel* (Experimental Bomber Squadron) created earlier in April became the 4th Squadron of this air force unit.

The operations flown by Ju 52s on the most active front at that time, the Madrid front, began on November 18 with a number of bombing raids against various military targets on the outskirts of the capital city. These operations continued daily, with the bombers flying a number of sorties against enemy

Airfield
After the arrival of the modern Heinkel 111s, the Junkers were relegated to a transport role.

THE ROLE PLAYED BY THE AIR FORCE

Junkers
Above and profile. These aircraft were camouflaged with three shades of paint: tan, gray and green. The blue saltire cross in the center of the fuselage was not usual.

Maintenance
Mechanics servicing the BMW engines fitted to the Junkers Ju 52.

Service ribbons
Below and over page. Among the service ribbons from Germany we can see some earned in Spain as a member of the Legion Condor.

positions, until the 22nd when Nationalist troops made their deepest penetration into the defensive cordon surrounding Madrid. On the 18th, in cooperation with aircraft of the same type belonging to the Nationalist Air Force, they attacked the airfield at Alcalá de Henares, inflicting severe damage while coming under heavy anti-aircraft fire and attacks from enemy fighters.

Loading bombs
Left. Ground staff loading bombs onto the Ju 52's vertical racks.

Plate
Below. Nice souvenir of the owner's sojourn in Spain during the Spanish Civil War as part of the German unit.

But the missions involving Legion Condor aircraft over the Madrid front were not the first, since on November 15, 16 and 17, Ju 52s had bombed the ports of Alicante and Cartagena. In the latter raid several vessels at anchor there were damaged – one was even sunk – and the port facilities suffered severe damage. On November 25 the German bombers returned to attack Cartagena again, inflicting serious damage to its facilities.

On the 27th, several Ju 52s were sent to the Andalusian front to carry out supply and ground support duties, mainly for the Civil Guard which was besieged in the Santa María de la Cabeza monastery and at Lugar Nuevo in the province of Jaén.

The Role Played by the Air Force

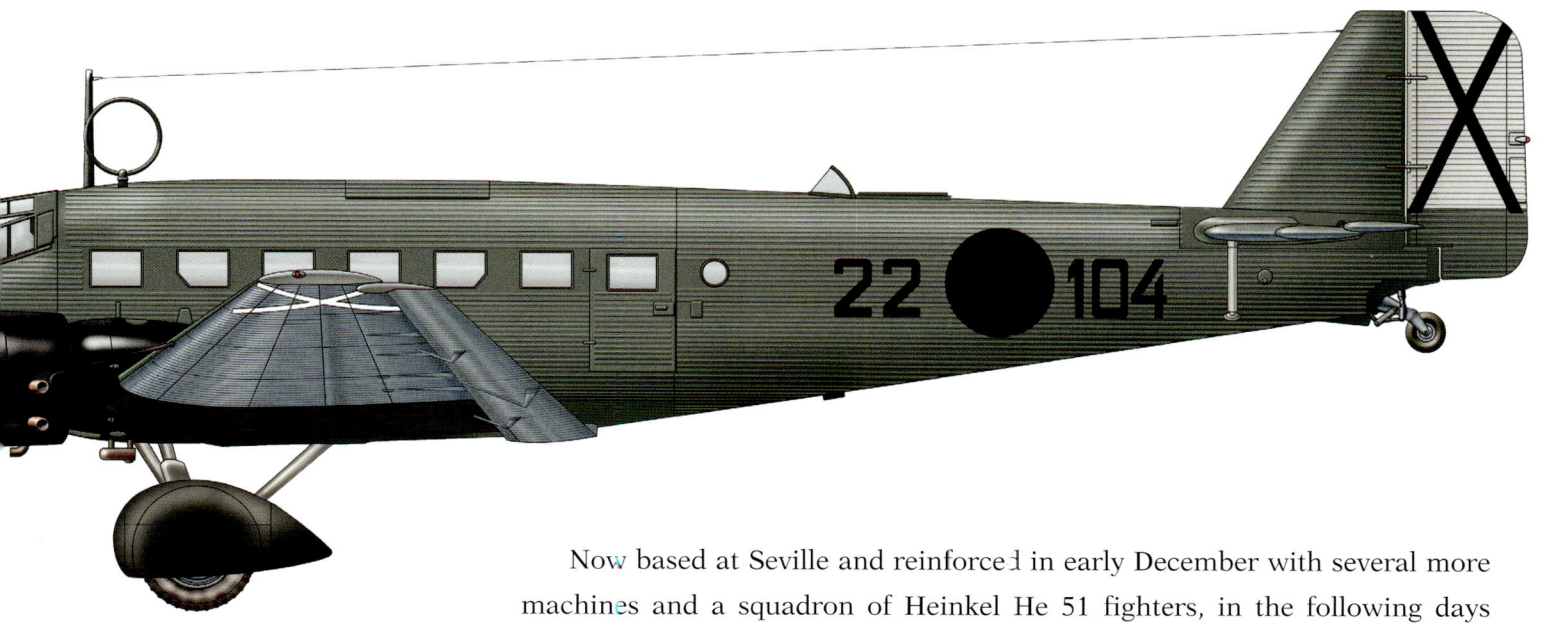

Profile
The latest Ju 52s to join the Legion Condor came without bomb racks.

Paperweight
Center, right. Emblem of K/88 which would later be used by the Luftwaffe during the Second World War.

Mail
Below. By half way through the conflict the Junkers 52 was used as a mail, personnel and freight carrier.

Now based at Seville and reinforced in early December with several more machines and a squadron of Heinkel He 51 fighters, in the following days the aircraft flew a number of sorties to drop food and medical supplies to the besieged troops, and also to bomb the enemy positions surrounding the monastery. After several days flying these missions, the three-engined Junkers returned to their base at Salamanca, although in early January 1937 they would fly south again to continue supporting the Nationalist troops which were attempting to advance towards the besieged Santa María de la Cabeza monastery. They made numerous bombing raids against enemy positions before returning to Salamanca on the 7th once the front had stabilized after the enemy advance had been halted.

Accident
Below. The Ju 52 was a very robust aircraft. In this case the aircraft "only" suffered a broken undercarriage.

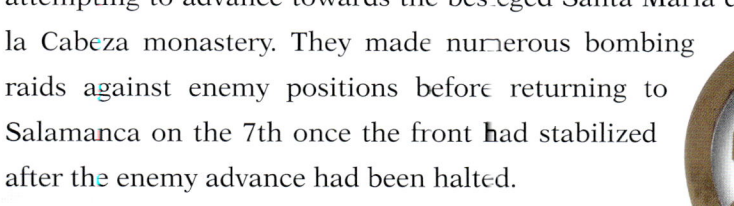

Häning
Junkers Ju 52 assigned to 2.K/88, nicknamed Häning. It bears the emblem of the squadron, a white eagle holding a swastika in its talons.

On February 25 the bombers of K/88 once again flew south, on this occasion in order to try to destroy the airfield at Andújar, which Republican aircraft were using as a base to pound repeatedly the defenders of the monastery. Their mission was fully accomplished.

In February 1937 the fierce Battle of Jarama was fought during which K/88 aircraft cooperated with the Nationalist Air Force in raids against enemy targets, mainly communications and airfields in the vicinity of the fighting although also attacks were also made against the Republican rearguard.

Song
Below, left. Words of the march composed in honor of the Legion Condor's bomber unit.

4.K/88
Alongside the Junkers Ju 52s, the twin-engined Heinkel He 111s of the disbanded VB/88 formed part of Squadron 4.K/88, which adopted this as its emblem.

Lied der K/88

Wir flogen jenseits der Grenzen
mit Bomben gegen den Feind,
hoch über der spanischen Erde
mit den Fliegern Italiens vereint. Refrain:

Die Roten sie wurden geschlagen
im Angriff bei Tag und bei Nacht,
die Fahne zum Siege getragen
und dem Volke der Frieden gebracht. Refr:

Wir kämpften an allen Fronten
als Deutsche in spanischen Reih'n,
um Kämpfer für Spaniens Freiheit
und Sieger für Deutschland zu sein. Refr:

Refr.: Wir sind deutsche Legionäre,
die Bombenflieger der Legion,
im Kampf um Freiheit und um Ehre,
Soldaten der Nation.
Vorwärts Legionäre!
:,: Vorwärts im Kampf sind wir nicht allein
und die Freiheit muß Ziel uns'res
Vorwärts Legionäre!:,: [Kampfes sein.

Oblt. Schlecht

German pilot
Badge belonging to Luftwaffe pilot. Strangely the German pilots in Spain only wore the regulation badge of the Spanish military air force.

Leutnant
Above. Pilot officer of a Ju 52, photographed with a fellow airman in the cockpit of his plane.

On March 9 the first twin-engined Heinkel He 111s (nicknamed *"Pedros"*), which had been delivered to the Legion Condor the previous month and formed part of VB/88 – the Experimental Bomber Squadron – received their baptism of fire when they attacked the airfields at Alcalá de Henares and Barajas. Subsequently all the squadrons of Bomber Group K/88 were to have their Ju 52s gradually replaced by these more modern aircraft.

Journey
Nearly all of the flying units of the Legion Condor had three-engined Ju 52s as "errand runners."

An einem neblichen Januar-Tag, flog ein Maschine unserer Staffel gegen einen

Meine Maschine wird beladen mit 50 Kilo Bomben. Die Front in La Cenia war so nahe, dass wir bei gutem Wetter sehen konnten wenn unsere Maschinen ihre

Ruhepause auf dem Leitwerk

Die He. 111 vom Heckstand aus gesehen

Brandbombenlager.

Ein neuer Liegeplatz-Schupp entsteht

„Me. 108"
(Kurier-Maschine der Gruppe)

Wagenpark meiner Staffel
3./K. 88

Führerstand der ...

„We. 34"
Unser Kurier-Flugzeug

Mit stehenden Motoren not-gelandet!

Wandmalereien in der Kantine   Unsere Kantine

Neues Jahr 1939

Meine Maschine startet

Neues Jahr 1939

Die Einsatzglocke

Unsere "Ju.52" (rechts auf dem Bild) holt uns wieder ab von "La Cenia" nach "Zaragoza"!

Cockpit
German pilots in the cockpit of a Junkers Ju 52.

In preparation for the Nationalist Army's offensive on the Northern front in late March, most of the German units were moved closer, setting up bases at Burgos and Vitoria. These two airfields were home to a total of twenty-five Ju 52s of Group K/88 which, from the very first day of operations (March 31), flew a great many bombing missions against enemy vanguard and rearguard positions, as well as attacking a number of communications nodes and the airfields where the few aircraft the Basque government could still muster were stationed.

In the next phase of that campaign, the advance on Cantabria, the airfields of Santander were systematically punished, as were the pockets of resistance in the main manufacturing centers of the province, mainly Reinosa and Torrelavega.

Badge
Some German pilots wore this badge on their uniform.

Heinkel He 111
Right. After VB/88 was disbanded its aircraft formed part of 4.K/88.

Heinkel He 111
Below. The red winged bomb was the emblem of 3.K/88. In the photo, two Sd.Kfz.7s and a Ju 52 belonging to this unit.

The Role Played by the Air Force

Bomber
Front view of a twin-engined He 111B, in which the forward machine gun and the Daimler-Benz engines are clearly visible.

Bombing up
Below right. The Heinkel He 111 was one of the best bombers of its time. In the photo we can see how bombs were loaded onto this aircraft.

Cockpit
Below left. Detailed profile of the nose of a Heinkel 111B in which we can see the cockpit and the forward machine gun position.

Finally, to complete the occupation of the entire Cantabrian coast, on September 1 the last Nationalist offensive was launched. In Cantabria resistance was far more serious than it had been in the two provinces previously captured on that front.

The aircraft of K/88 (formed by four squadrons – the 4th was the former VB/88 – two equipped with Junkers Ju 52s and the other two with Heinkel He 111s) were entrusted with the role of bombing coastal targets, airfields and ports that were vital to the enemy supply lines. The port of Gijón, the most important of the area, suffered several raids, in one of which, specifically the one on October 20, the He 111s sank the destroyer *Císcar*.

LEGION CONDOR

Plate
Above, left. This plate probably belonged to Group K/88's services unit.

Early in July of that year, the Republicans had launched a strong offensive in the Madrid sector with the idea of halting the enemy advance in Vizcaya. Air and ground forces of the Legion Condor were also involved in the engagement known as the Battle of Brunete, sent hurriedly from the Northern front for that purpose.

From July 9 the German squadrons were used to bomb repeatedly and continually, by day and by night, enemy lines of communication, troop concentrations and airfields in the area. The latter raids had the vital effect of immobilizing enemy air units and helped overturn the advantage that the Republican air force had enjoyed during the early days of the offensive. A total of two Ju 52s were lost in the course of the battle. Once the battle was over, on July 26 the German aircraft were flown back to the Northern front to resume their activity in support of a fresh advance on Santander.

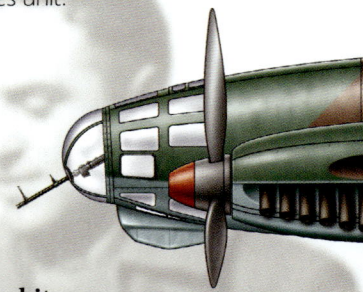

Flying kit
Below, left. This German airman is wearing a flying suit with a sheepskin collar and a regulation Luftwaffe flying helmet.

Inside an He 111
Center. The observer/bomb aimer of a He 111 had an excellent field of vision that helped him do his job effectively.

Bracelet
A German made this bracelet using the pilot and Spanish observer's emblems.

The Role Played by the Air Force

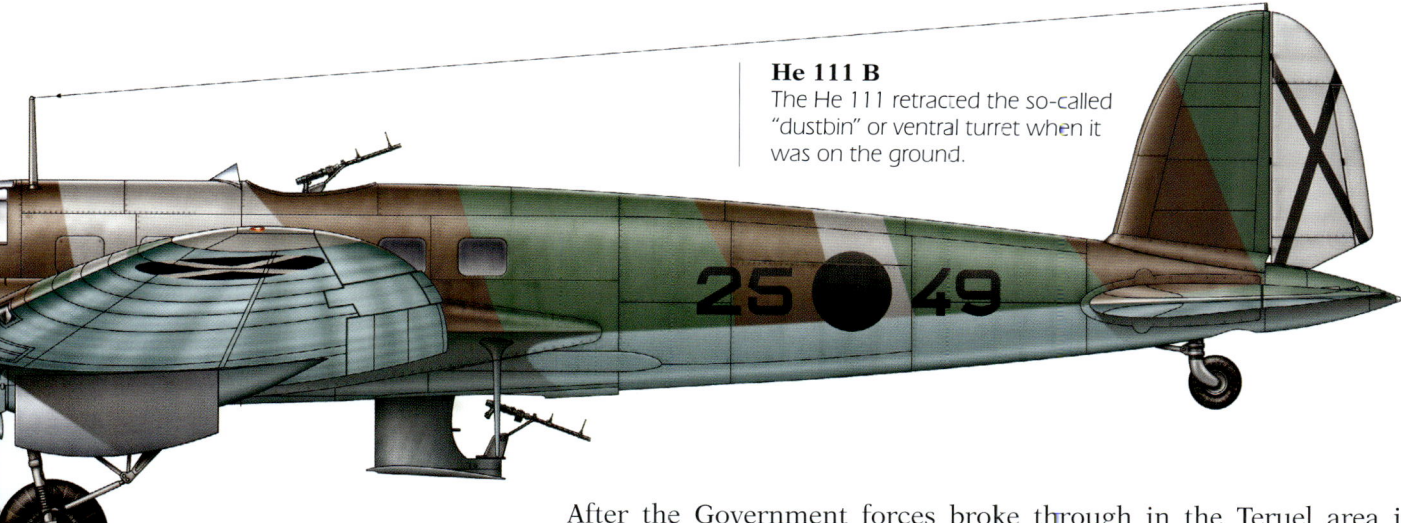

He 111 B
The He 111 retracted the so-called "dustbin" or ventral turret when it was on the ground.

Inspection
Previous page, below. A number of mechanics are photographed working on the wing of a He 111 in a hangar.

Winged bomb
This emblem was inherited by the He 111 from its predecessors in 3.K/88, the Junkers Ju 52.

After the Government forces broke through in the Teruel area in mid-December 1937, the various air force units of the Legion Condor were sent to the sector to help halt the enemy advance and thwart their plans. Group K/88 took part in this operation and, when the harsh weather conditions allowed, heavily bombed the enemy positions. The Group lost one He 111 in this action.

The next offensive launched by the Nationalist high command was the advance towards the Mediterranean, starting from Aragon and crossing the *Maestrazgo* mountain range. The breakthrough along the front was achieved on March 9, 1938 and the German bombers pounded the enemy fortifications. Some days later, the squadrons of the Group moved their base to the Sanjurjo airfield in Zaragoza when the Nationalist plans for the offensive were changed, and the Segre basin became the new destination. By now the bombers were operating practically without opposition since the Republican fighters could offer no serious resistance.

Legion Condor

"The war is over"
Above. These bombs were probably never used, given the date and the message on the board.

About this time, on April 17 to be precise, 34 He 111s of K/88 made two raids on the port of Cartagena and one on the port of Almería as part of what was known as "Operation Neptune." The port facilities and the vessels that were at anchor in the port suffered serious damage (at Cartagena the battleship *Jaime I* was hit). Only one of the Heinkel He 111s was hit by anti-aircraft fire defending Cartagena although it was not shot down. It tried to return to base along the coast but while flying over Almería it was again hit by anti-aircraft fire defending that port. This time it was shot down; the aircraft crashed into the sea near Motril but the crew managed to bail out. The next day the aircraft that had not suffered any damage flew back to base at Zaragoza.

Pedros
Center, left. The Heinkel He 111 inherited its nickname from their predecessor, the Junkers Ju 52.

The Role Played by the Air Force

After cutting the Republican zone in two, the Nationalist offensive pushed on towards Valencia along the Mediterranean coast. By this time several Spanish pilots were attached to K/88 as reinforcements since the group, along with other Legion Condor units, was seriously understrength.

Sanjurjo Airfield
Above, right. Heinkel He 111 parked at Sanjurjo Airfield (Zaragoza).

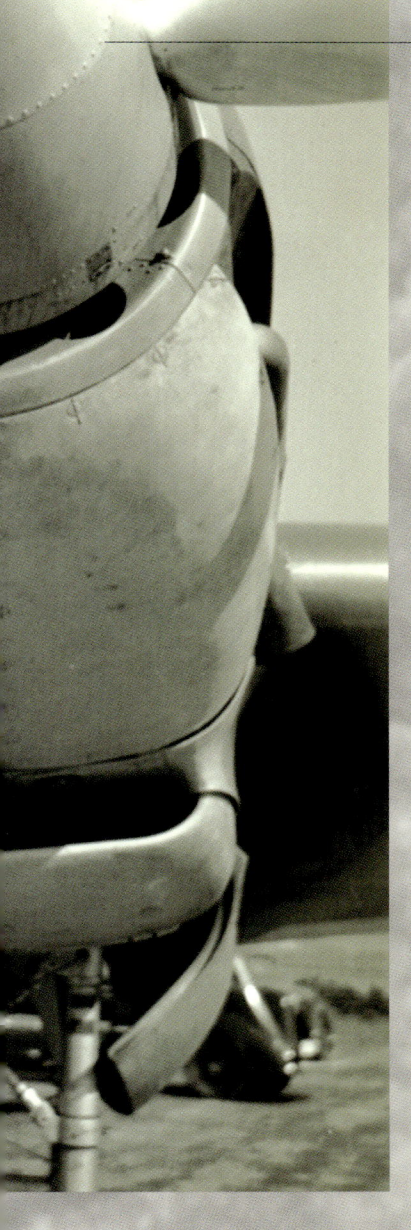

Engine
Center. Detail of the engine, radiator and retracting landing gear of a He 111.

Twin-engined
He 111 belonging to the fourth squadron of K/88 (4.K/88)

Camouflage
Above. The wing of this He 111 – flying over a village somewhere in Spain – shows perfectly how the camouflage scheme of Luftwaffe aircraft worked in Spain.

In the early hours of July 25, Republican troops crossed the Ebro at several points and smashed through the Nationalist defenses set up on the river's right bank. Thus began the most important and bloodiest battle of all those fought during the fratricidal conflict. From the first days of the enemy attack the He 111s of the Legion Condor were used to relentlessly bomb the Republican positions, as well as the Mediterranean ports, airfields and communication nodes of their rearguard. During the months of fierce fighting, the Group's losses could be considered to be very light given the number of sorties flown by its aircraft.

The next phase of the conflict was the Nationalist Army's offensive against Catalonia, which started on December 23, 1938. For this operation K/88 started out

Decorative plate
Below, left. Members of 1.K/88 had this decorative plate made with the German, Italian and Spanish pilot badges round the outside and the unit's emblem in the middle.

Emblems
Over page, above. Two personal emblems on two Heinkel He 111s. The four-leaf clover was on 25•12.

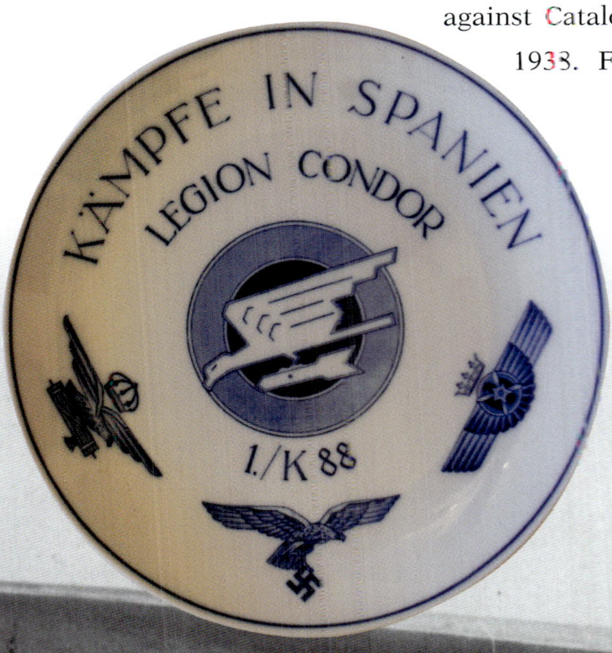

Granuja
This Heinkel He 111 has the word *"Granuja"* (Grifter) painted on its side; a very Spanish word for a very German aircraft. In front we can see the bomb racks used by these aircraft.

THE ROLE PLAYED BY THE AIR FORCE

with forty He 111s (according to Hidalgo Salazar), which operated alongside Spanish and Legion air forces bombing the targets they were assigned. By now they practically had no fighter opposition to fear, although enemy anti-aircraft artillery was still very active.

On March 12, 1939 the bomb load of a Heinkel He 111 of 1.K/88 exploded over the Madrid municipality of Vicálvaro. The entire crew of the bomber perished, as did the Group's commander, *Oberstleutnant* Härle, who was on board at the time. These were the last human losses in action suffered by K/88, and also by the Legion Condor as a whole.

Personal emblem
Below. Many of the aircraft of K/88 bore special and unique emblems, painted by their crews, as in the case of the plane in this photo.

Lapel
Right. A variant of the emblem of 2.K/88. It is a lapel badge belonging to an unidentified airman.

LEGION CONDOR

THE ROLE PLAYED BY THE AIR FORCE

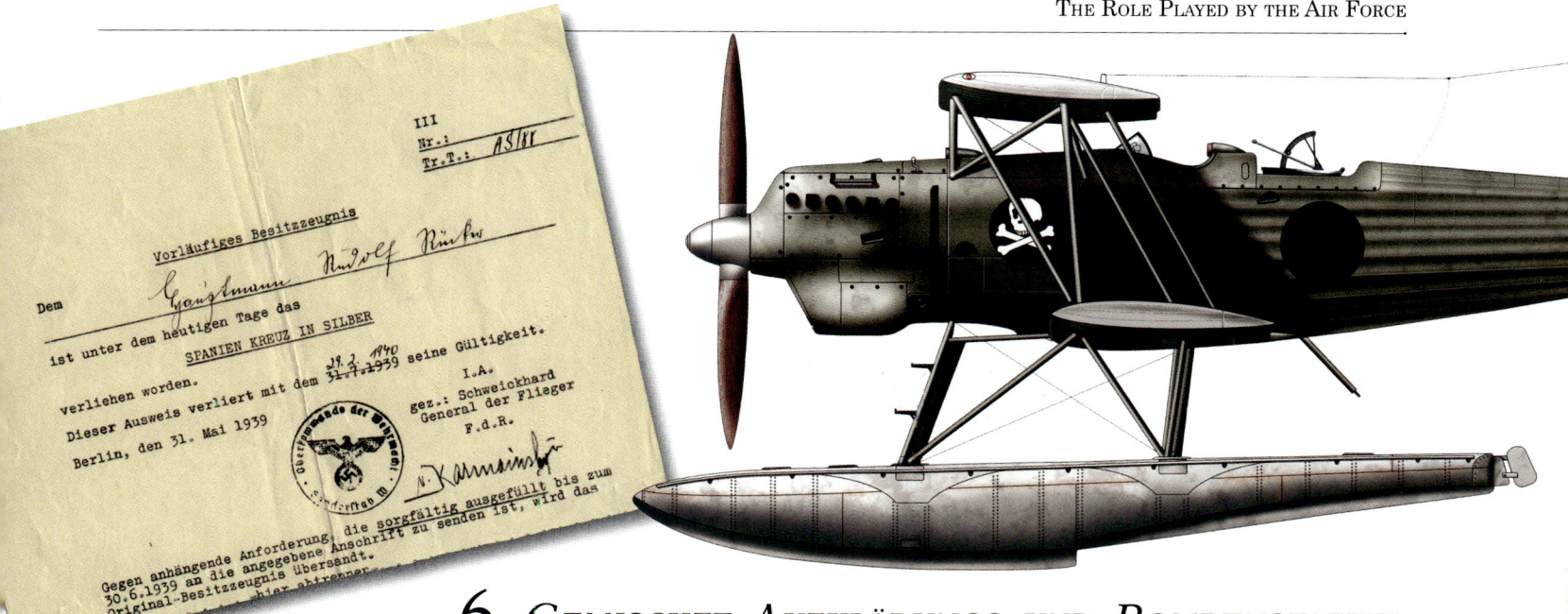

Heinkel He 60
Above, right. The emblem of the first He 60 seaplanes was a white skull and crossbones on a black background. These aircraft were given three figure numbers instead of the regulation codes.

Award
Above, left. Certificate of the award of the Spanish Cross in silver to a member of AS/88.

6. GEMISCHTE AUFKLÄRUNGS UND BOMBENSTAFFEL (SEE), AS/88. MIXED NAVAL RECONNAISSANCE AND BOMBING SQUADRON

The first two German Heinkel He 60 seaplanes arrived in Spain in October 1936 and were immediately assembled in the factory at Puntales (Cadiz). They began to operate out of that naval base, mainly on reconnaissance and light bombing missions along the Mediterranean coast. Notable actions in this period included the attacks on the enemy airfield at El Rompedizo (Malaga) and the shooting down of an enemy Breguet XIX over the coast of Malaga.

A little later came the twin-engined Heinkel He 59s and these and the He 60s mentioned earlier were the regulation aircraft of Squadron AS/88 that was set up when the Legion Condor was officially formed. The first commander of this unit was *Hauptmann* Karl Heinz Wolf. The German seaplanes continued their maritime reconnaissance sorties and their attacks on enemy merchant shipping from their port of Cadiz base.

Sea Wolf
The first three Heinkel He 60s were given somewhat pompous names. 513 was called "Sea Wolf" while the other two were called "Sea Beast" (512) and "Sea Terror" (511).

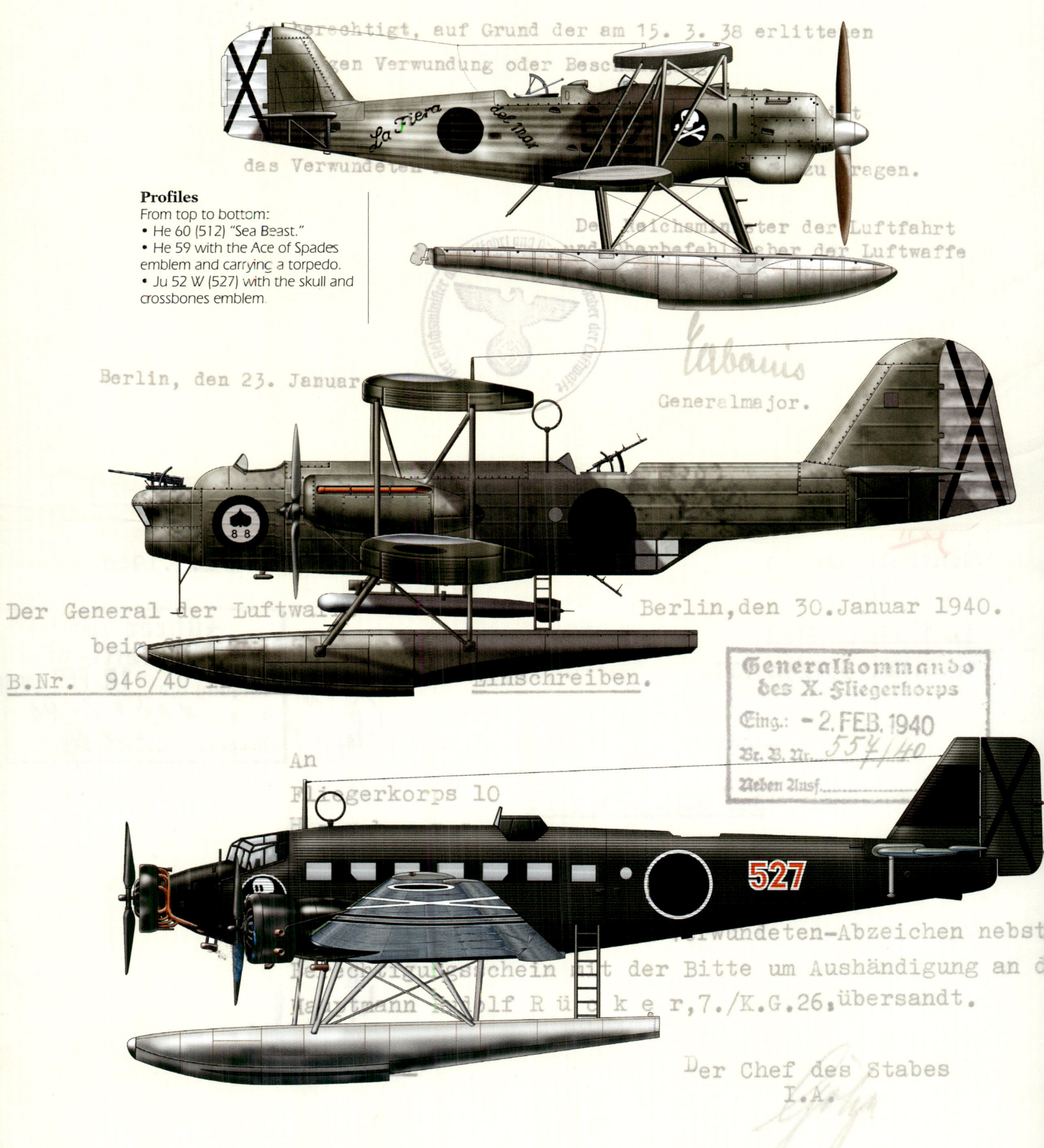

Profiles
From top to bottom:
• He 60 (512) "Sea Beast."
• He 59 with the Ace of Spades emblem and carrying a torpedo.
• Ju 52 W (527) with the skull and crossbones emblem.

The Role Played by the Air Force

Sea Beast
This seaplane had to be hoisted on board the cruiser "Canarias" after an accident during the Malaga campaign. Detail of the "Totenkopf" emblem used by the aircraft of AS/88 early in the war.

Early in 1937 the German seaplane unit had a successful involvement in the offensive launched by the Army of the South against Malaga. In this campaign the squadron suffered its baptism of fire when two seaplanes collided as a result of an attack by enemy fighters.

AS/88 was next stationed at the port of Melilla and later had a fleeting stay at Malaga once the city fell into Nationalist hands.

Durante this period *Hauptmann* Günther Klünder took command and Horten torpedoes started to be used for the attacks on enemy naval movements in the Mediterranean, combined with the use of bombs of different weights. In May 1937 a Heinkel He 59 succeeded in shooting down an enemy Dornier Wal.

Legion Condor

Personnel of AS/88
Most of the German personnel of AS/88 had their photo taken at the Pollensa air base (Mallorca), which was the squadron's operational base port for most of its operational life in Spain.

In the summer of 1937 at the request of Nationalist Air Command, Squadron AS/88 was moved to the Balearic Islands and set up its permanent base at Pollensa on the east coast of Mallorca. The reason behind this move was to take part in the air-sea blockade of the mainland Levante coast where the Republican's most important trading ports were, as well as the major naval bases at Cartagena and Mahón (Menorca).

Under the command of *Hauptmann* Hans Hefele the German seaplane unit began to make frequent night bombing raids on ports, from the north of Catalonia to the province of Almeria. It also specialized in the harassment of Republican coastal railways and truck traffic on roads, using cannon fire and incendiary bombs. At the same time the unit was continuing to attack the so-called "pirate ships" of any nationality and this triggered more than a few diplomatic incidents, especially with Great Britain and France.

Twin-engined seaplane
Below, left and profile. Heinkel He 59 (529) with the typical skull and crossbones below the cockpit. This particular aircraft is carrying a Horten torpedo.

THE ROLE PLAYED BY THE AIR FORCE

Launch
Above. The launch "Pollensa" used as a support and aircrew rescue vessel for the seaplanes based at Pollensa.

Torpedo
Right. Detail of the "Horten" torpedo tube, ventrally mounted on one of the He 59s.

As from January 1938, Squadron AS/88 was led by *Hauptmann* Martin Harlinghaussen, soon to be promoted to *Major*, and this commander remained at the head of his unit for nearly a year, during which time he chalked up some notable successes and was decorated as a result. The last man to command the squadron was *Hauptmann* Helmer Smit, who took charge of it in January 1939 and remained as its leader until the war ended.

On the beach
This He 59 is beached on the Mediterranean coast. On its side it carries the characteristic pennant of the "Non-Intervention."

In the course of the war the German seaplane unit was equipped with twenty-seven Heinkel He 59s, five Heinkel He 60s and one three-engined Junkers Ju 52 W fitted with floats, as well as two Heinkel He 115s that arrived at Pollensa on March 26, 1939, four days before the end of the conflict. Another three Arado Ar 95 seaplanes ordered by the Legion Condor did not arrive in time to take part in the war and, once it was over, they were handed over to the Spanish Air Force.

Hoist
Pulling a Heinkel He 59 seaplane out of the water with a hoist at the Pollensa air base (Mallorca).

The Role Played by the Air Force

Ceremony
Personnel of AS/88 render military funeral honors to one of their comrades killed in action. The casket is loaded on board a Junkers Ju 52 W to be flown back to Germany.

In terms of materiel, AS/88 lost at least seventeen seaplanes, either Heinkel He 59s or He 60s, but on the positive side the unit succeeded in sinking or capturing forty-eight enemy merchantmen, accounting for a total tonnage of around 100,000 tons. Once the war was over, AS/88 handed over three He 59s and two He 60s to the Spanish Air Force. The rest of the air materiel was sent back to Germany, the only instance of this happening among Legion Condor units.

LEADERS OF AS/88 SQUADRON
HAUPTMANN KARL HEINZ WOLF (NOVEMBER 36-FEBRUARY 37)
HAUPTMANN GÜNTHER KLÜNDER (FEBRUARY 37-JULY 37)
HAUPTMANN HANS HEFELE (JULY 37-JANUARY 38)
HAUPTMANN MARTIN HARLINGHAUSSEN (JANUARY 38-DECEMBER 38)
HAUPTMANN HELMER SMIT (JANUARY 39-APRIL 39)

Bombs
Above and below. Ventrally sited cradles for 250 and 500 kilo bombs on twin-engined He 59s.

Horten
Launching torpedoes from He 59 seaplanes was tried out in Spain on several occasions with a relative degree of success.

Heinkel He 115
Over page, below. The latest seaplanes delivered to AS./88 were two moderns twin-engined Heinkel He 115s, which arrived too late to take part in the conflict.

THE ROLE PLAYED BY THE AIR FORCE

Nose cannon
Above. The 20mm Lb-201 cannon fitted to the nose of the He 59 was frequently used to attack enemy railway traffic along the Mediterranean coast.

Ace of spades
The definitive emblem adopted by AS./88 was the "Ace of Spades," which was seen in different forms.

The Role Played by the Air Force

Medals
German medal ribbon, including the 1936-1939 campaign medal.

St. Moreau
Previous page. The three types of aircraft that VB/88 was equipped with. This unit was also known as the *Staffel Moreau*, as the inscription on the badge shows. A just uncorked bottle of champagne was painted on the side of the Heinkel 111s as a mark of their success.

Heinkel
The first four He 111s to arrive in Spain were attached to VB/88, forming the first *Kette*.

7. *Versuchsbomberstaffel*, VB/88. Experimental bomber Squadron

Late in 1936, Legion Condor high command had realized that the air materiel they had was clearly technically inferior to what the Republicans were receiving from abroad, especially from the USSR.

To help redress this imbalance in the case of the Bomber Group, in mid-February 1937 a new squadron was formed, made up of a number of the Luftwaffe's most modern aircraft, with the idea of testing them under actual combat conditions. Four Heinkel 111 B-1s, four Dornier 17 E-1s, and four Junkers 86 D-1s arrived in Seville from Germany to form what was to be

Legion Condor

known as the Experimental Bomber Squadron (*Versuchsbomberstaffel* – VB/88). Command of this unit was given to *Oberleutnant* Rudolf von Moreau, one of Germany's most experienced bomber pilots who had been in Spain since August 1936. As well as the military flying crews and the ground staff who looked after them and their aircraft, a group of civilian specialists from the firms of Junkers, Heinkel, Dornier, Mercedes and BMW were also sent to Spain.

FUMO
Above, left and profile. The Junkers Ju 86 was fitted with Jumo 205C diesel engines and failed to meet expectations. While the Spanish called them "Jumo" the Germans painted the word "Fumo."

Pablo
Center. The Dornier Do 17s of VB./88 were nicknamed "Pablo."

The Role Played by the Air Force

Accident
Left. Heinkel He 111 25•3 was transferred from VB./88 to 4.K/88, as the emblem on the fuselage shows.

The aircraft of this new unit mainly saw action in operations over the Northern front, although they also attacked targets on other fronts.

In the months following the squadron's formation new aircraft of the above-mentioned types were received and some were lost in bombing raids against enemy positions and airfields.

Late in August 1937, what had until that moment been considered to be the Legion's Experimental Squadron was transferred to the following.

Pendant
Above, right. With the three flags of the Axis countries, plus the Spanish flag.

Fuselage
The disassembled fuselage of Ju 86 26•3 is transported to the Leon Depot on the back of a truck.

Cigarette case
Right. Another damascened piece from Toledo, very sought after by the members of the Legion Condor.

Legion Condor

Angelito
The Legion Condor's first dive-bombing unit was equipped with Henschel Hs 123s. The aircraft coded 24•2 carried the *Totenkopf* emblem on its fuselage.

8. *Stuka Kette 88.* "Stuka" DIVE-BOMBING FLIGHT

This unit started its operational life on the Southern front, equipped with Henschel Hs 123 "Angelito" aircraft. It was absorbed into J/88 when the experimental unit coded VJ/88 was disbanded, and operated out of the Tablada airfield, Seville, and Cordoba airfield early in 1937. In March, the unit was moved to the Madrid front where it suffered its first loss, before going north to Vitoria airfield under the orders of *Leutnant* Heinrich Brücker, where it operated over the Vizcaya front.

Its main purpose was to take out enemy artillery positions by means of dive-bomb attacks using medium weight bombs. *Stuka Kette* 88 would suffer another two losses, both by ground fire, in the course of operations in the Bilbao area.

Once the Northern campaign was over, the two surviving aircraft were handed over to the Nationalist Air Force and the unit was disbanded.

In February 1938 the first operational Junkers Ju 87 A arrived in Spain. Under the command of *Leutnant* Hermann Haas they were incorporated into Fighter Group J/88 as its 5th Squadron (5.J/88), making its debut in the Battle of Alfambra.

The unit served in the Aragon, Levante and Ebro campaigns, mostly operating out of La Cenia airfield,

Ju 87 A
They were the first Stukas of this type to operate in Spain. *Unteroffizier* Bartels piloted aircraft 29•2.

The Role Played by the Air Force

In flight
Previous page, above. A Ju 87A in flight over Spanish soil.

Ju 87 B
Above and below, right. The Ju 87Bs of K/88 made their debut during the Catalonian operations in the winter of 1938-1939

attacking specific targets such as communications nodes, bridges and minor fortifications.

Practically at the end of the Battle of the Ebro, 5.J/88 was disbanded when its aircraft were sent back to Germany to be serviced. The Catalonian campaign saw the rebirth of this unit, once again as *Stuka Kette* 88, but this time it was attached to Bomber Group K/88 and equipped with the new Junkers Ju 87 B. This unit, led by *Hauptmann* Bohne, served until the end of the war, suffering at least two losses, one from anti-aircraft fire and another by a Republican fighter. Once the war was over the aircraft were all sent back to Germany.

29•5
Profile and below, left. The Stuka 29•5 was the last of this type to arrive in Spain. The emblem of the unit, the pig *Jolanthe*, was painted on the wheel fairings.

THE ROLE PLAYED BY THE AIR FORCE

Emblem
Some W 34 aircraft were painted with a frog motif, alluding to their meteorological role.

Junkers W 34
The 43•1 was crewed by civil meteorologists seconded to K/88.

9. *WETTERSTELLE*, W/88. WEATHER UNIT.

When the Legion Condor was formed in November 1936 it was assigned three Junkers W 34 Hi weather aircraft. These were single-engined, fixed undercarriage aircraft fitted with meteorological measuring and sounding equipment that were assigned the type-number 43 and coded 43-1, 43-2 and 43-3. At least the second of these aircraft had a green frog in a white circle painted below the cockpit, the same emblem carried by the Junkers Ju 52 3m coded 22-80, perhaps also used for weather reconnaissance duties.

Their first base was the Tablada airfield outside Seville where these aircraft flew daily meteorological reconnaissance sorties to provide weather forecasts for the pilots of the Legion Condor.

Weather aircraft
Above and below, right. The Junkers W 34 was mainly used to fly weather reconnaissance missions to protect combat aircraft.

The German pilots and meteorologists were militarized civilians and by way of anecdote we reproduce below the diary entry for January 2, 1937 of one *Oberleutnant* Otto Winterer, a pilot assigned to experimental monoplanes of VJ/88 who went on to become squadron leader of fighter squadron 2.J/88:

"There has been another scramble. Without engaging in combat, because the enemy bombers turned back before they reached Seville. I still haven't had any contact with the enemy.

"There are problems with the civilian staff. They are infected with communist ideas. Trautloft amuses me a lot with his radiant humor.

"Ironies of the principles or fundaments of Nazism and the power of the bourgeoisie. The weather airmen are paid more than an *Oberleutnant* who is serving in the front line: 3,500 marks compared with 1,200 marks.

Accident
Right. Junkers aircraft made of corrugated metal were very robust in the event of an accident.

Transport
Right and center. A total of eight Junkers W 34s arrived in Spain. Not all were used as weather aircraft: some were used as transport planes.

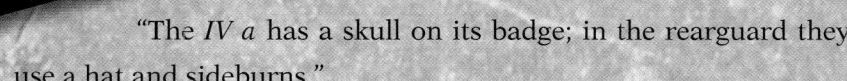

"The *IV a* has a skull on its badge; in the rearguard they use a hat and sideburns."

Shortly afterwards, two of the Junkers W 34 weather aircraft, those coded 43-1 and 43-2, were assigned to *Stab* K/88. Their respective crews comprised the civilian pilot Haep and Dr. Nitze (meteorologist), and the engineers Schulze-Eckart (pilot) and Krug (meteorologist). Apparently, the aircraft coded 43-3 was assigned to *General* Gonzalo Queipo de Llano, commander of the Army of the South, for use as a personal transport aircraft.

Later, and until July 7, 1937, another three Junkers W 34s were sent to Spain, either to cover losses in the weather unit or to be used by the Legion Condor Staff as liaison and personnel transport aircraft.

Weather aircraft continued to be attached to Bomber Group K/88, mainly based at the airfields of Burgo de Osma (Soria) and later Zaragoza.

At the end of the Civil War, three Junkers W 34s were handed over to the Spanish Air Force.

La Cenia
Below. W 34 weather aircraft operated at practically all the airfields where operational units of the Legion Condor were stationed.

Barajas
The signals unit of the Legion Condor (Ln/88) during the Barajas parade, in May 1939.

Spanish Cross
Certificate of the award of the Spanish Cross in bronze with swords to an officer attached to signals.

10. LUFTNACHRICHTEN-ABTEILUNG (MOT.), LN/88. MOTORIZED SIGNALS BATTALION

Although it is a little known unit, its activity was of undeniable importance.

The first *Luftnachrichtentruppe* (signals troops) to arrive in Spain were the three radio operators on board the freighter *Usaramo* together with the other eighty-three volunteers of the Armed Forces of the Reich who arrived at Cadiz in the early hours of August 6, 1936.

Most of their equipment arrived on the freighters *Camerún* and *Wilberg* between late August and the early days of September. From the month August, the signals unit was under the orders of *Oberstleutnant* Ingo Lindner.

Third company
Below. Vehicles of 3./Ln88 in operation.

Krupp
Above and center. Krupp L3 H163 signals truck.

Telephones
Below. Telephone linemen belonging to Ln/88.

When the Legion Condor proper was formed, within this unit the *Luftnachrichtenabteilung* 88 (Ln/88) or Air Signals Battalion was set up, comprising four companies plus a staff company. This battalion was led by *Major* Kurt Schubert.

The first men of this battalion arrived in Cadiz on November 15 on board the steamship *Fulda* and by December 2 the unit was up to full strength, both in terms of men and equipment.

Various sections were distributed between Seville, Salamanca and the Madrid front, mainly to set up telephone exchanges, radio stations, telex exchanges,

Cufflinks
Pin and damascened cufflinks of 1./Ln88

The Role Played by the Air Force

Direction finding
Right. Sd.Anh. 422 trailer with direction finding equipment.

Marble plaque
Above. In memory of a member of Ln/88 in bronze and marble.

Very modern equipment was used in Spain by Ln/88, such as direction finders, radio beacons and radiophares, as well as radio telephone equipment for ground to air communications. The experience gained by the members of this unit would stand them in good stead in the world war to come.

Bretón Theater
Previous page, below. The Bretón Theater in Salamanca served as the headquarters and barracks for Ln/88.

Büssing-NAG
Büssing-NAG Type G 31(Kfz.61) signals truck.

F/88

Flak 30
Left. 20mm light anti-aircraft gun defending an airfield.

Plaque
Center. Made of wood and tin, this plaque is decorated with a bas-relief of a Flak 88mm cannon.

Zaragoza
In the parade held at the Sanjurjo airfield we see three anti-aircraft guns belonging to F/88: a 37mm Flak 18, an 88mm Flak 18, and a 20mm Flak 30.

11. *Flakabteilung (Mot.)*, F/88. Motorized anti-aircraft battalion

Prior to the formal organization of the Legion Condor, on August 6, 1936 the merchantman *Usaramo* docked in Seville with a small detachment of twenty 20/65mm Flak 30 light anti-aircraft cannon, which is the number Franco had initially asked Germany for in his first request for military aid. It is probable that on August 31, also in Seville and also aboard the *Usaramo*, the first heavy Flak battery arrived with a full complement of men and equipment. This shipment included the Mod.36 firing control, the real driver of the effectiveness of the system, and four state-of the-art Krupp 88mm Flak 18s. The battery was commanded by *Leutnant* Aldinger, which led to it being known for a long time by this officer's surname. This gun was to be used for the first time in Spain. It came to be known worldwide as the "eight eight," but its legend was forged in the war in Spain.

LEGION CONDOR

Heat
Two Germans manning a 20mm anti-aircraft gun scan the horizon in search of enemy aircraft.

Ribbons
Below. The *Unteroffizers* of the Legion Condor wore these ribbons on their breast and headgear.

The Aldinger Battery was first set up at the Seville airfield (Tablada), where it was soon combat ready and being used to train the first Spanish anti-aircraft gunners.

A few days after the talks held between *General* Franco and *Admiral* Canaris, on October 30, 1936 Berlin authorized the formation of a corps of volunteers of the *Luftwaffe* (assigned the number 88), together with other elements of the army (*Heer*) and the navy (*Kriegsmarine*), to support Nationalist Spain. By the end of November, the Legion Condor already had a significant amount anti-aircraft cover, provided by *Flakabteilung* 88 and commanded by *Oberstleutnant* Hermann Lichtenberger, although it was still awaiting the incorporation of various shipments of men and materiel. Its composition was as follows:

Flak 18
Over page. Artwork by Ramiro Bujeiro representing an 88/56 Flak 18 gun and crew.

COMPOSITION
THREE HEAVY BATTERIES (*SCHWERE*) OF 88/56 FLAK 18 CANNON NUMERADAS 1ª, 2ª AND 3ª.
TWO LIGHT BATTERIES (*LEICHTE*) OF 20/65 FLAK 30 CANNON
ONE BATTERY OF SEARCHLIGHTS (THE 6TH)
ONE AMMUNITIONS COLUMN

ID cards
Belonging to members of F/88. One German and the other Spanish.

Flak 18
Previous page. Light 37mm Flak 18 gun, portrayed by Ramiro Bujeiro.

Plaque
Belonged to a member of the 2nd Battery F/88.

First operations of the German anti-aircraft battalion in Spain

We know little about the first actions of the Flak units in Spain. Spanish archives only mention that on December 28, as part of operations on the Madrid front, and due to having to move the bulk of the Legion Condor's aircraft from the flooded airfield of San Fernando to the one at Encinas (province of Avila), *General* Hugo Sperrle, head of the Legion Condor, asked for anti-aircraft cover to be provided by a battery of 88s. Surviving documentation reveals that at that time there were only four batteries of that caliber (plus the two 20mm batteries): the one at Seville, the one at Salamanca (to protect the *Generalísimo*'s headquarters), and two more near the front to protect the ground units. At the beginning of 1937 the 6th battery of the Legion Condor was converted into a heavy searchlight and sound locator battery. Some months later the ammunition column, reinforced with human and material resources, would become the 7th battery. Meanwhile, the Aldinger Battery was attached to F/88 as its 8th battery.

Group F/88 fought at the Battle of Jarama, which started on February 5, 1937. After the unfortunate result of the Battle of Guadalajara, which paralyzed the attack on Madrid, and the reorganization of the Legion Condor on March 29, 1937, the group moved northwards to take part in the Vizcaya offensive.

Defense of La Cenia
Full crew of a light 20mm Flak 30 defending La Cenia airfield.

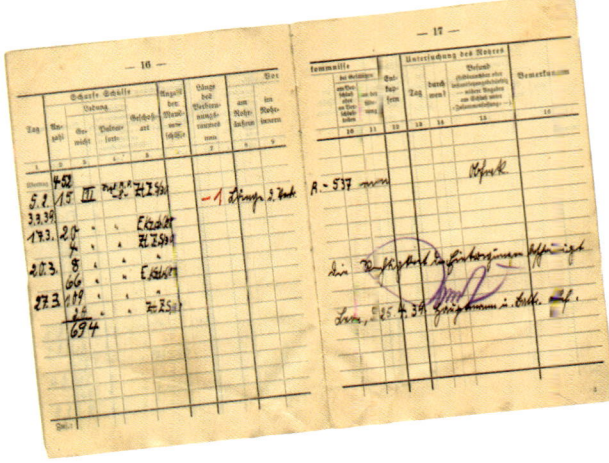

The pattern of combat of Group F/88 in Vizcaya was characterized by few anti-aircraft duties and regular deployment as ground artillery, for which role it was in great demand due to the ease with which it could be transported over difficult mountain roads and tracks by powerful conventional and half-track trucks and, of course, due to the accuracy of its guns against strongholds. We also know that the 88mm Flak 18s took part in the assault on the Iron Belt, as did the 20mm Flak 30s, which were taken right up to the front line, as a result of which they suffered several casualties due to badly placed Italian bombs. Once the Battle of Brunete was over, and in order to continue with the Santander campaign, on July 29 the Legion Condor transferred to the Aguilar de Campoo sector (Palencia). As its presence was not deemed necessary to halt the Republican offensive on Belchite, the Legion Condor continued operating in the Asturias campaign, advancing from west to east in early September.

Artillery Gun Book
Above, left. Refers to an 88mm anti-aircraft gun. The last entry was in Leon on April 24, 1939.

Levante
Above, right. One of F/88's heavy cannons, emplaced somewhere on the Levante front.

Machine gun
Over page. Crew of a 20mm Flak 30 machine gun on the Catalonia front.

Shield
Unofficial shield of the 8.F/88

Ground targets
Below. The 88mm artillery pieces were often used to knock out ground targets.

Close-in defense
Above, left. MG 15 machine guns from the First World War were used for this purpose.

Hygiene
Above, right. The soldiers on campaign washed and shaved in the most practical manner possible.

Reorganization of F/88 and Offensives in Aragon

Once the war in the North was over there was a period of reorganization and rest lasting a month, in which time the commander of the Legion Condor was relieved. As part of this reorganization, two sections of automatic 37mm Flak 18 (37/57) cannon were added to the Group, each of the existing light batteries receiving one section.

F/88's participation in the initial stage of the Battle of Teruel is not clear. Between January 4, 1938 and the 12th of that same month, dispatches of F/88 start to mention the fighting. The anti-aircraft role is mentioned practically every day as is the batteries' now familiar role as ground artillery.

Watchfulness
Right. This gun crew is on the lookout for a possible enemy air attack.

Introduction

Colonel
The most notable commander of the F/88 was Hermann Lichtenberger who led the group from August 1937 to April 1938.

Medals
From above to below: Spanish Cross in Gold, Campaign Medal, and War Cross.

The Legion Condor's anti-aircraft group took part in the Aragon offensive, which the Nationalist Army launched on March 9, 1938 in support of the *General* Yagüe's Moroccan Army Corps. The 88/56 anti-aircraft guns took part in the spectacular advance made by the 5th Navarre Division on March 12 between Belchite and Escatrón, the village where there was the fiercest resistance, with its tanks and assault aviation to the fore. This was a successful trial run of what would shortly be known as Blitzkrieg. Once the Aragon offensive had been completed on April 18, 1938, when Nationalist forces reached the Mediterranean at Vinaroz, F/88 took part in the Levante campaign, providing the Galician Army Corps with three heavy batteries and one light battery of the Legion Condor. After May 25 F/88 was reorganized to cover the following combat roles:

Sanjurjo airfield
Above, left. 88/56 heavy anti-aircraft gun at the airfield near Zaragoza.

88/56
Above, right. The Legion Condor's anti-aircraft guns remained in Spain after the end of the war.

ORGANIZATION
SUPPORT AND PROTECTION OF THE GALICIAN AC: 2 HEAVY BATTERIES AND ½ LIGHT BATTERY
PROTECTION OF THE COMMAND POST AT BENICARLÓ: 1 HEAVY AND ½ LIGHT
PROTECTION OF LA CENIA AIRFIELD: 1 HEAVY AND ½ LIGHT
PROTECTION OF THE PORT OF VINAROZ: 1 HEAVY AND ½ LIGHT

THE ROLE PLAYED BY THE AIR FORCE

Fuses
Left. The photo shows AZ 28 adjustable fuses, used in 88mm shells.

Framed map
Previous page, center. A volunteer's souvenir of his time spent in the 4th Battery (light) of F/88.

Drinking cup
Below, right. Silver cup belonging to a gunner of the fourth anti-aircraft battery of the Legion Condor.

German
20mm Flak 30 light anti-aircraft gun emplacement

F/88 in the Battle of the Ebro and the Catalonian Campaign

The Battle of the Ebro started at dawn on July 25, when the Nationalist divisions were poised to press on to Valencia, while in Europe the Sudetenland crisis was at its peak. The 50th Division of the Moroccan Army Corps manning the zone under attack was overrun and it was necessary to fill the breach with units hurriedly taken from other fronts, a decision which caused the immediate paralysis of the Levante offensive. The Republican advance was halted on July 29 outside Gandesa. Along a 35km front the attackers had penetrated to a maximum depth of just under 25km, an area of about 600 km² between the rivers Matarraña and Canaleta. The territory won included mountainous areas (the Fatarella, Pandols and Caballs ranges) that would become famous because of the fighting that ensued in order to reclaim the lost ground.

On July 29 the batteries of F/88 which had previously been supporting the Galician Army Corps took up positions on this new front, to the south of the main bridgehead (Gandesa, Pandols, Río Canaleta), in support of the 4th and 84th Divisions, having abandoned the Levante front. By August 5 the enemy forces had been contained and the front stabilized, whereupon a battle of attrition would ensue until October 29.

Legion Condor

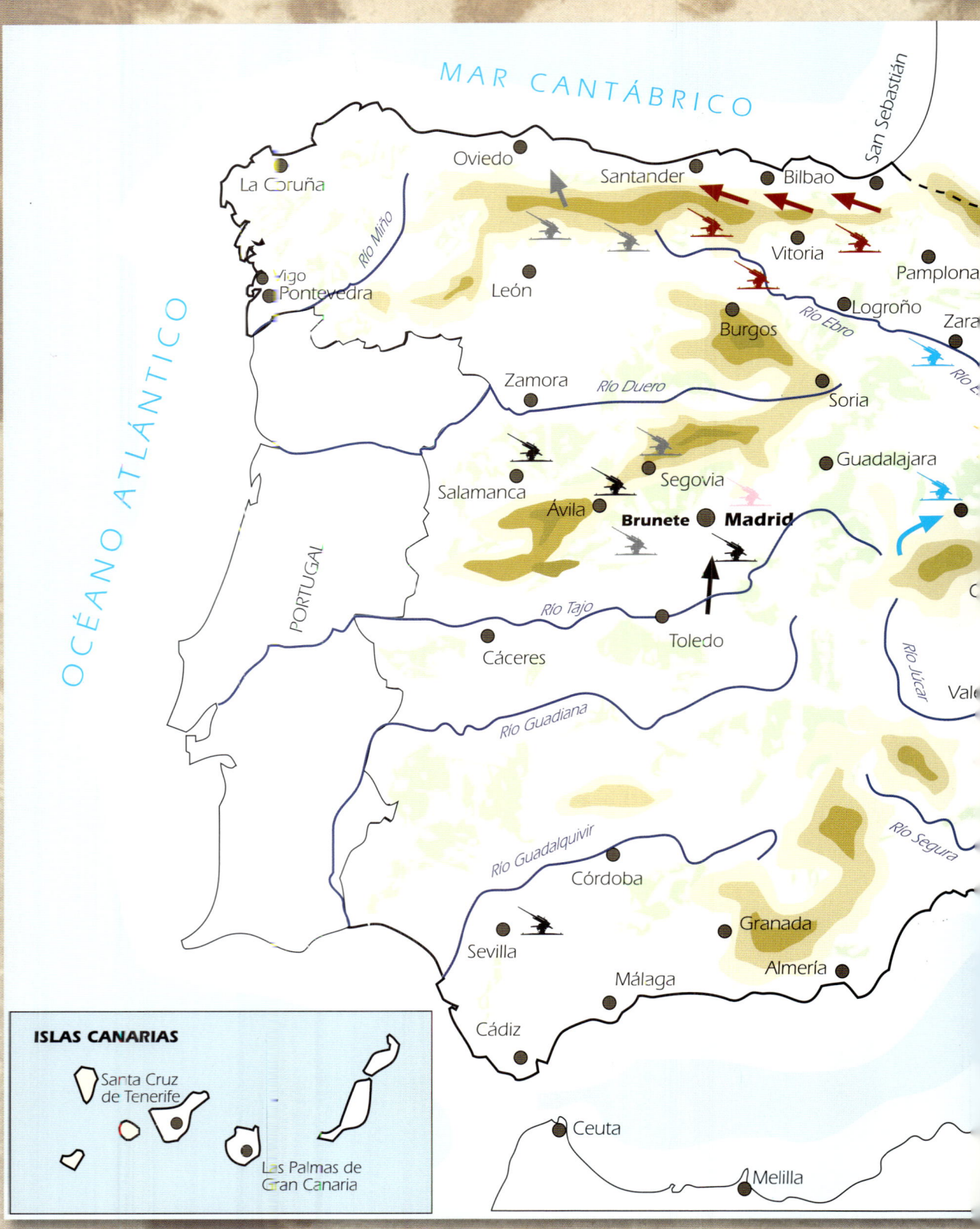

The Role Played by the Air Force

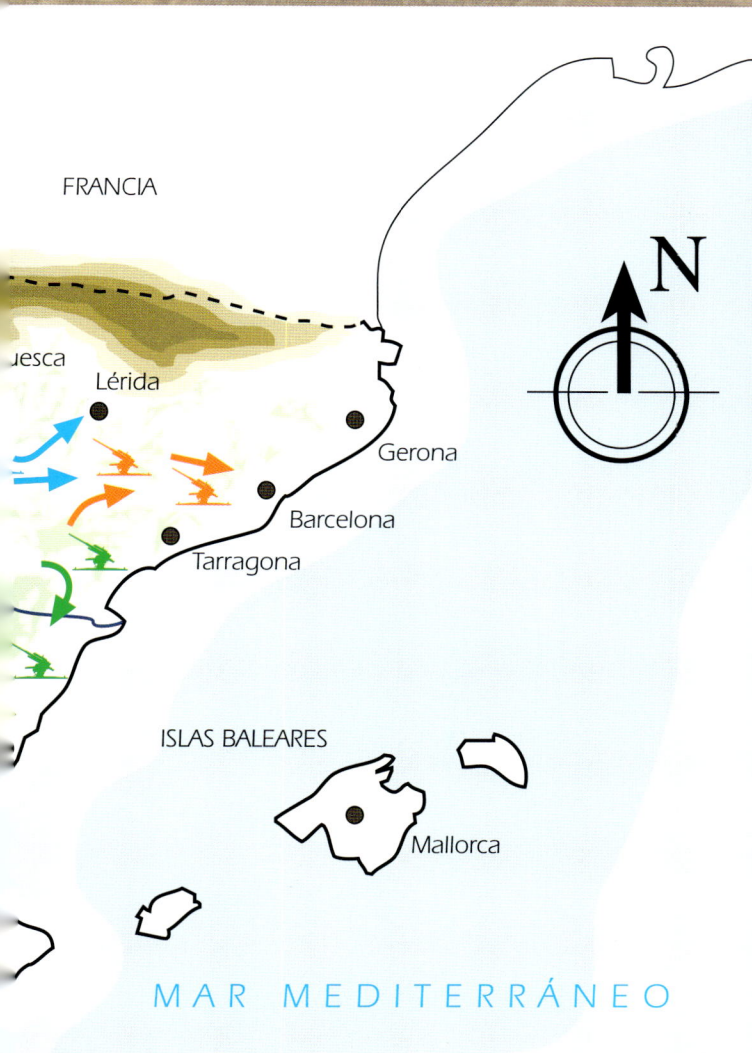

LEYENDA
- Primeras operaciones. Nov. 36 - Marzo 37
- Campaña del Norte. Ofensiva sobre Bilbao. Marzo - Junio 37
- Brunete y Santander Julio - Octubre 37
- Campaña de Aragón y Teruel Nov. 37 - Abril 38
- Campaña de Levante Abril - Julio 38
- Batalla del Ebro Julio - Nov. 38
- Campaña de Cataluña Dic. 38 - Feb. 39
- Ultimas operaciones Marzo 39

German volunteer
German *unteroffizier* wearing a slouch hat.

Commander
Oberst Georg Neuffer, Chief of Staff of F/88 between April and September 1937.

After the Battle of the Ebro concluded on November 16, 1938, about a month passed before the Catalonian campaign began. On December 23, the Urgel and the Maestrazgo Army Corps broke through the enemy lines at the bridgeheads of La Baronía and Tremp. The Legion Condor, with its bases at the airfields of Sanjurjo, La Cenia and Zaidín and its command post at Almacellas, was entrusted to support the Navarre and the Moroccan Army Corps while also carrying out night bombing raids. In January just the Navarre Army Corps was being supported.

At the end of the war, in March 1939, the composition and commanders of Group F/88 were as follows:

Sd.Kfz 7
Above. Twelve ton half-track for towing heavy guns.

37mm anti-aircraft gun
Center. Only two sections of these peculiar anti-aircraft cannons arrived in Spain

STAFF OF F/88 IN MARCH 1939
COMMANDER: *OBERST* ERICH KRETSCHMANN
1ST HEAVY BATTERY OF 88/56 MM FLAK 18, *HAUPTMANN* BUNDT
2ND HEAVY BATTERY OF 88/56 MM FLAK 18, *HAUPTMANN* REUTER
3RD HEAVY BATTERY OF 88/56 MM FLAK 18, *HAUPTMANN* VON JABLONSKI
4TH LIGHT BATTERY OF 20/65 MM FLAK 30, *HAUPTMANN* VOGEL
5TH LIGHT BATTERY FLAK OF 20/65 MM FLAK 30, *OBERLEUTNANT* WEHLA
6TH SEARCHLIGHT BATTERY, *OBERLEUTNANT* HÜBENER
7TH AMMUNITION BATTERY, *LEUTNANT* JACOBI
8TH HEAVY BATTERY OF 88/56 MM FLAK 18, *LEUTNANT* HACKER
9TH HEAVY BATTERY OF 88/56 MM FLAK 18
TOTAL: TWENTY 88 MM FLAK 18, TWENTY-EIGHT 20 MM FLAK 30, AND SIX 37 MM FLAK 18

The Role Played by the Air Force

Cup of F/88
Three views of a commemorative cup belonging to a soldier of F/88. Note the inscription of the places where he served.

Orders dated March 1939 regarding operations aimed at breaking through the Central front called for supporting action by four batteries of F/88. In this final period of operations, on March 24, the 1st, 2nd and 3rd Batteries of F/88 were positioned to the east of the Ermita de Bastilla, with the job of protecting the Navarre Army Corps. Thus they ended the war alongside the men of the former "Navarre Brigades" with whom they had practically started the war.

The F/88 lost a total of thirty-three killed in action or in accidents in Spain. The group took part in the great military parade at Barajas (Madrid) and in the Victory Parade held in the *Paseo de La Castellana* boulevard of the capital city. After bidding farewell to the city of Leon, which had such a strong allegiance to the Legion Condor, on May 24 F/88 boarded the *Wilhelm Gustloff* bound for home, leaving practically all its materiel in Spain.

Iron Belt
German gunners of an 88mm anti-aircraft crew pose with a shell of that caliber during the operations leading to the penetration of the Iron Belt.

Commemorative plaque
Made in wood and metal, this was a common souvenir among F/88 gunners.

THE ROLE PLAYED BY THE AIR FORCE

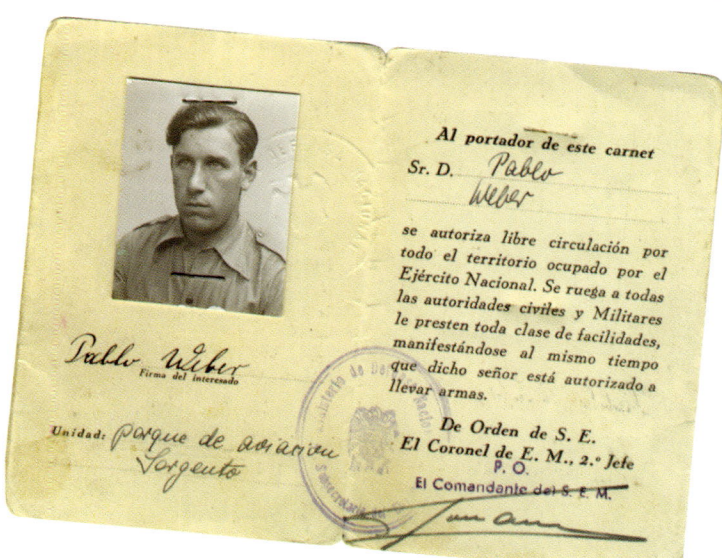

ID card
Spanish documentation of a sergeant of the Depot Group of the Legion Condor.

12. LUFTZEUGGRUPPE UND LUFTPARK, P/88. AIR MAINTENANCE GROUP AND DEPOT

The first German fighter aircraft, the Heinkel He 51, which arrived in Spain by sea in August 1936, at the port of Cadiz, were assembled at the South Regional Depot at Tablada airfield, Seville. The other German aircraft that were to arrive on various German vessels as the war progressed, such as the experimental Henschel Hs 123, Heinkel He 50 and Junkers Ju 87 dive-bombers, and the first three prototypes of the Messerschmitt Bf 109 V fighter, not to mention the Heinkel He 112 V, were also all assembled at the Tablada workshops, by German technical staff sent over by the manufacturers and military mechanics of the *Luftwaffe* from the Rechlin Test Center.

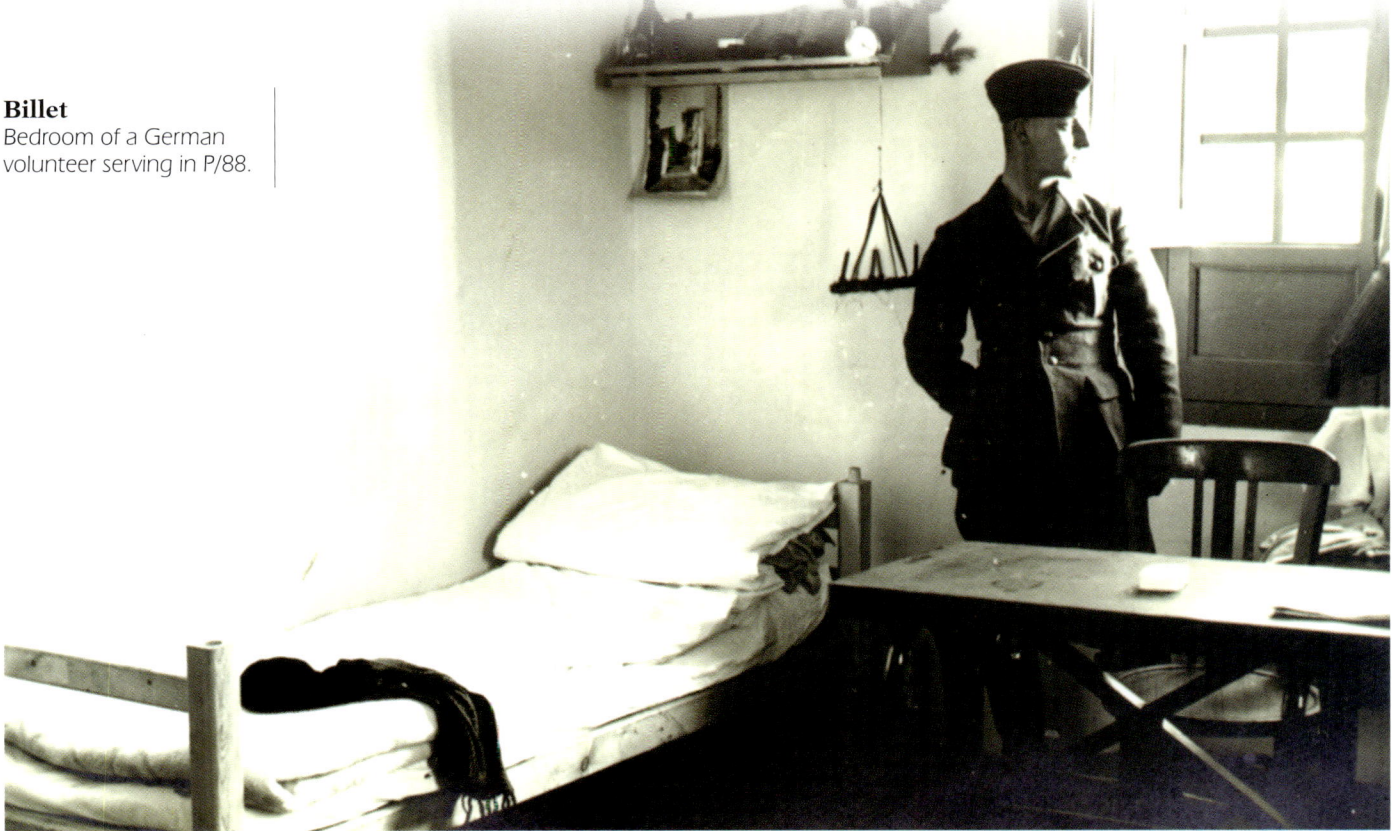

Billet
Bedroom of a German volunteer serving in P/88.

Office
The Depot Group employed various personnel – both civilian and military – to meet its administrative needs.

When the Legion Condor was officially formed a depot unit was created, called P/88, whose initial base was, unsurprisingly, at the Tablada airfield near Seville. This unit comprised three companies, called 1.P/88, 2.P/88 and 3.P/88, the second of which was largely composed of militarized civilian staff; that is, workers similar to those of the Spanish *Maestranza* depot.

After the arrival of the first modern twin-engined aircraft which were to form the experimental squadron VB/88, consisting of Heinkel He 111s, Junkers Ju 86s and Dornier Do 17s, we know the names of some of the German engineers sent to oversee the assembly of these aircraft. We know that Dornier sent to Tablada *Dipl.Ing.* Junginger and that Gerd Klein-Schmeink was the on-board engine test engineer at this time.

Vehicles
This German functionary controlled the vehicles assigned to the Depot Unit.

Special vehicles
Heavy vehicles and trailers belonging to P/88, used for transporting materiel for the various units of the Legion Condor.

After the start of the Northern campaign and the transfer of practically the entire Legion Condor to airfields close to the Cantabrian coast, P/88 also relocated, leaving Seville to set up on the site of the former Northwest Regional Depot at the Virgen del Camino airfield in Leon. It was there that the new batch of Messerschmitt Bf 109 fighters earmarked for Squadron 1.J/88 were assembled before making their maiden flights in the Santander campaign. Once the Battle for Asturias was over, with the fall of Gijón on October 21, 1937, all the Legion Condor's air materiel was serviced and repaired at the Leon Depot and several aircraft were handed over to the Spanish, such as the Heinkel He 70s, Henschel Hs 123s and Junkers Ju 86s, not to mention the three-engined Junkers Ju 52s.

Anti-aircraft defense
7.92mm machine gun used for close-in defense of P/88.

Switchboard
German Legionnaire responsible for P/88's switchboard.

Once P/88 had set up base in Leon, the German vessels carrying the aircraft to Spain changed their ports of landing to La Coruña or Vigo in Galicia, in order to facilitate shipping by road or rail to Leon.

At this time the head of the Legion Condor depot unit in Leon was *Major* Schomburg, aided by the clerk, Zischka. As early as February 1938, the first Junkers Ju 87A (Stukas) were assembled at Leon and made their debut in the last days of the Battle of Alfambra, on the Teruel front.

Throughout 1938 the Leon Depot continued to assemble Heinkel He 111s, Messerschmitt Bf 109s and Dornier Do 17s, as well as performing the regular

Bunk beds
Dormitory for troops of the Legion Condor's Depot Group. In the foreground we can see gun racks for rifles.

THE ROLE PLAYED BY THE AIR FORCE

Platform signs
Above, left. The railway station at La Virgen del Camino served P/88.

Officers' mess
Above, right. Two P/88 officers read newspapers in the officers' mess.

Column of P/88 Group
Below. A column of heavy trucks, laden with large crates containing parts of various aircraft in service.

maintenance work on Legion Condor aircraft and repairing and rebuilding German aircraft damaged in combat.

The P/88 Depot Unit remained in Leon for the rest of the conflict and, as can be imagined, played a vital role in the preparation of the events organized in the city to give the Legion Condor a proper send-off at the end of the Civil War.

Its contribution to the final victory was very important, since as well as assembling, repairing and servicing aircraft, its staff helped train Spanish aeronautical specialists.

CHAPTER III

The Role Played by Ground Forces: Imker-Gruppe

1. IMKER-DROHNE, PANZERGRUPPE "THOMA"

Panzer I
Above. Birdseye view of a Panzerkampfwagen I Ausf.A tank, sent to Germany to form the Nationalist armored unit. (Julio L. Caeiro)

On September 23, 1936, the commander of the 2nd Batalion of Panzer-Regiment 4, based at Schweinfurt, *Oberstleutnant* Wilhelm Ritter von Thoma, was urgently sent to Spain. The *Heer* high command had ordered him to take command of the armored training group that would soon be embarking, bound for Spain. Three days previously, on September 20, 1936, all the officers, NCOs and soldiers of the two battalions forming Panzer-Regiment 6 had been assembled at the Neuruppin base, where the commanders, there and then, called for volunteers to take part in an important mission abroad. They warned their subordinates that this would not be a mere exercise or maneuvers, but that there would be actual fighting and that they could be taken prisoner, be wounded or even killed.

Digging
A number of Germans recently arrived at Cáceres are digging trenches near the Arguijuelas castles, headquarters of the *Gruppe Thoma*.

Legion Condor

Nearly all the men stepped forward and volunteered for that secret mission outside Germany; a romantic adventure for some and a good opportunity to put into practice the tactics learned during so many months for most.

Once the men were selected the contingent was organized and the tanks of the type that was, at that time, the standard one for the unit, the Panzerkampfwagen I Ausf. A, were prepared, as well as various types of vehicles, trucks and motorcycles and their corresponding weaponry.

The volunteers were transported to Döberitz, on the outskirts of Berlin, where they received a special payment to cover their immediate expenses and the cost of civilian clothing. Also, during their time spent away from Germany, they temporarily ceased to belong to the *Wehrmacht* since it was necessary not to

In Avila
Above, right. A break in the journey to admire the landscape: Avila's city walls.

Medals
Above, left. Set of medals belonging to a German Legionnaire.

Plaque
Over page, above, right. Plaque in wood and metal commemorating the German Panzer units.

Field kitchen
Field kitchens were normally transported on trucks.

Daily chores
Soldiers of *Gruppe Thoma* sawing a log near their barracks.

Tank men
Hauptmann Heinz Wolf (left), commander of the 2nd Tank Company of *Gruppe Thoma* next to one of his men.

officially commit German troops to a foreign conflict. The German tank crews, fitted out with civilian clothing and false passports, looked like a youthful but oddly homogenous group of travelers waiting to set off on their summer holidays under the hot sun of a country that, at that time, they knew nothing about. The group was taken by road to Stettin, a port city where they would board ship, heading for an uncertain destiny. On September 28, 1936, the panzer unit settled aboard the merchantmen *Passajes* and *Girgenti*, which were also carrying their gear and all the materiel required to perform their duty at their point of destination.

Skull and crossbones
Badge worn on the front of the berets of German tank crews of the *Drohne* Group.

Illustration
An illustration by Ramiro Bujeiro featuring the Group Commander, *Oberst* von Thoma (left), the commander of the 1st Tank Company, *Oberleutnant* Gerhard Willing (center) and an *unteroffizier* of the *Panzergruppe* in the turret of a Panzerbefehlswagen I Ausf.B.

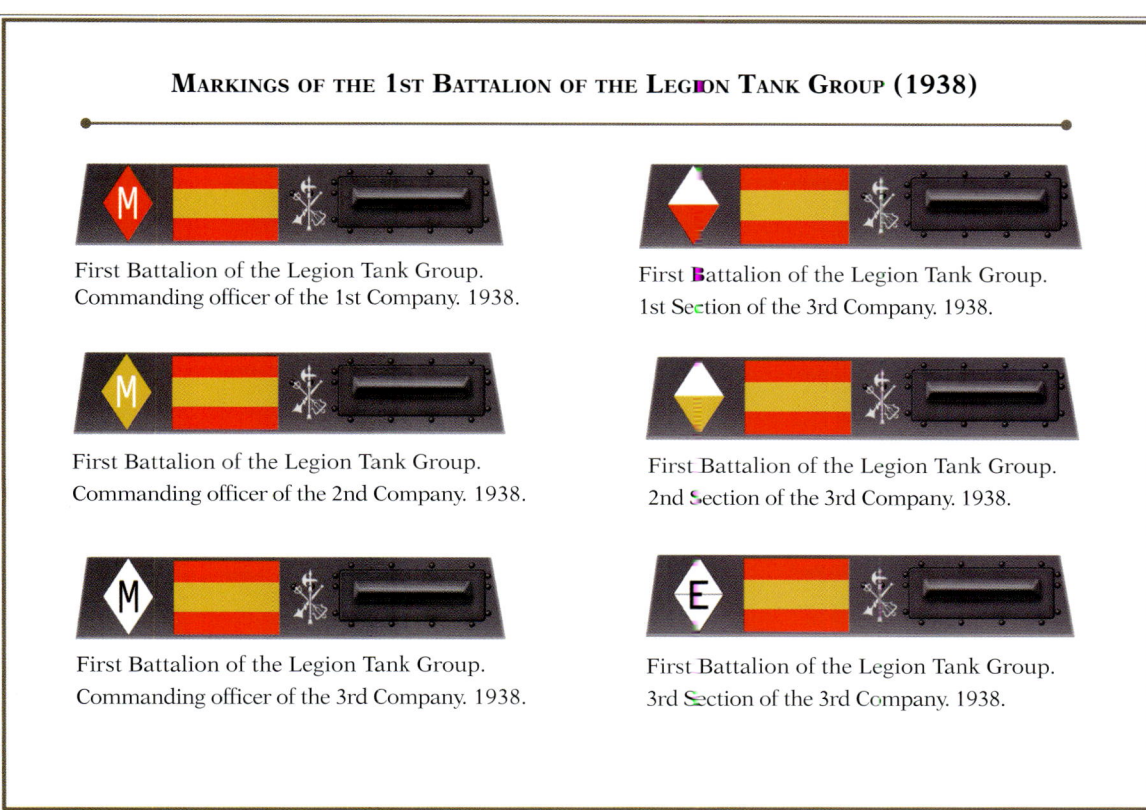

The expedition was formed by 267 men, the complement of the *Panzergruppe* staff, two complete tank companies, one transport company, one workshop company, one ammunition company and an anti-tank gun training unit. They took with them forty-one Panzerkampfwagen I Ausf.A tanks, ten Büssing-NAG 80 trucks for towing tank transporter trailers, six mobile workshops, eleven light automobiles, forty-five heavy trucks (including fourteen Vomag tank transporters), nineteen Sd.Ah.115 tank transporter trailers, and eighteen motorcycles, as well as twenty-four PaK 37mm 35/36 anti-tank guns and assorted accessories and spare parts.

Field kitchen
The Group's cook with some helpers preparing lunch.

Legion Condor

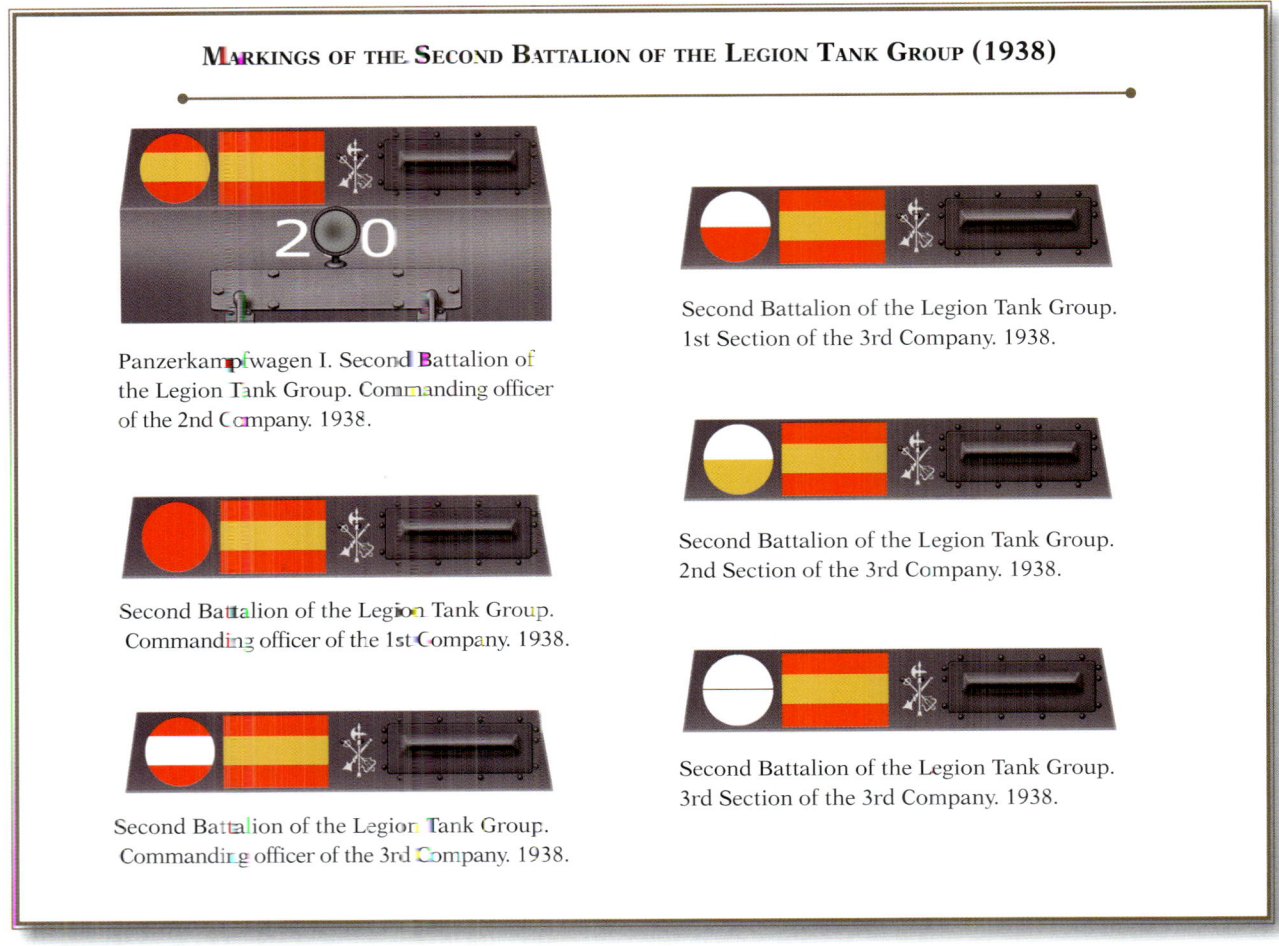

Markings of the Second Battalion of the Legion Tank Group (1938)

Panzerkampfwagen I. Second Battalion of the Legion Tank Group. Commanding officer of the 2nd Company. 1938.

Second Battalion of the Legion Tank Group. Commanding officer of the 1st Company. 1938.

Second Battalion of the Legion Tank Group. Commanding officer of the 3rd Company. 1938.

Second Battalion of the Legion Tank Group. 1st Section of the 3rd Company. 1938.

Second Battalion of the Legion Tank Group. 2nd Section of the 3rd Company. 1938.

Second Battalion of the Legion Tank Group. 3rd Section of the 3rd Company. 1938.

On October 7, 1936, the vessels entered Spanish waters and from that moment on they were escorted by the pocket battleships *Admiral Scheer* and *Deutschland* and the torpedo boat *See Adler*. As the day was ending they arrived at the port of Seville, where the men disembarked and the materiel was unloaded.

Soon after arriving in Seville, the Group was sent by railway to Cáceres in several journeys between October 8 and 10. A week later, on the 18th, the troops would be reviewed by Franco at their base at the castle of Arguijuelas.

Badges
Tank badges to be worn on the beret or on the tunic breast. At that time there was very little standardization with regard to uniform in the tank units.

Black beret
After the first few months, members of the *Gruppe Thoma* wore the same uniform as the rest of the Legion Condor, except for their headgear, which was a black beret.

The Role Played by Ground Forces: Imker-Gruppe

Loading up
Various members of the *Panzergruppe* are filling 7.92mm magazines.

By then *Oberstleutnant* von Thoma had already taken command of the unit, with *Major* Eberhardt von Ostman acting as his second-in-command and chief of staff.

During the month of November thirty-seven more men arrived who, together with their comrades already in Spain and twenty-one new tanks, in this case Panzerkampfwagen I Ausf.B from Panzer Regiment 4, which arrived in Seville on the 25th of that month on board the *Urania*, formed the 3rd Tank Company of the *Panzergruppe*. Meanwhile the group's command post moved to Cubas de la Sagra, a village in Madrid, where the training school and workshop were also set up.

Vehicle
Below. Staff car of *Gruppe Thoma*.

Transport
A Vomag Type 5LR 448 truck with an Sd.Ah.115 trailer carrying two Panzer I tanks.

If we take into account the casualties and the men who returned to Germany at various times, at the end of 1936 there were 299 German tank men in Spain. A year later there were only 124 and by the end of 1938 only 108 remained.

Between October 1936 and May 1939, von Thoma's men trained Spanish troops in such diverse subjects as tanks, anti-tank guns, flamethrowers, mine launchers, gas protection, maintenance, driving and ammunition handling.

Command tank
Above. Panzer I command tank being repaired at *Panzergruppe Drohne* workshop.

2nd Company
Below. Note the early uniform of the German tank instructors.

The Role Played by Ground Forces: Imker-Gruppe

Front panel
The Panzerbefehlswagen I Ausf.B was a type of command tank based on the Panzer I. The type that fought in Spain was a little different from the type that would be seen in the Second World War. (Julio L. Caeiro)

"Negrillo" tanks

A total of seventy-two were provided by Germany for the ground contingent to operate at the beginning of the war, sent to Spain in three separate shipments of forty-one, twenty-one and ten tanks, respectively.

As has already been mentioned, the first batch, comprising forty-one Panzerkampfwagen I tanks, arrived in October 1936 together with the personnel and the rest of the materiel. All the tanks received in this shipment, except for the command tank, were of the Ausf.A type, which in Spain were called *Krupp*.

The second shipment of German tanks arrived in Spain in late November 1936, and comprised twenty-one Panzer I's, probably of the Ausf.B type. In December fifteen of them plus one command tank were organized into the third company of the Nationalist Tank Battalion. Another five were set aside to cover losses. Finally, Legion Condor accounts mention a third delivery comprising ten Panzerkampfwagen I tanks, although neither the delivery date nor the version is clear. We would hazard a guess that the shipment may have been made in early 1937 to cover losses suffered up until then.

Badge
Previous page, center. Spanish tank badge used during the Civil War.

Von Thoma
On the right, *Oberst* Wilhelm Ritter von Thoma (with a black beret), with *Teniente Coronel* Asensio and various Nationalist officers. The photo was taken in the early days of the German group's stay in Spain since *Oberst* von Thoma is still wearing blue overalls with three horizontal stripes on the left sleeve as the only insignia.

Legion Condor

These then were the seventy-two tanks sent to Spain through the Legion Condor.

But their intensive use on the battlefield, the normal wear and tear of delicate and almost experimental equipment, and the losses suffered in the Spanish civil war meant that these sventy-two tanks were not enough to keep the unit operational. Therefore the Spanish military authorities asked Germany for more Panzers.

Captured T-26
The Nationalist armored units made use of many tanks captured from the enemy.

Profile
Soviet T-26B tank incorporated into the Nationalist army. (Julio L. Caeiro)

THE ROLE PLAYED BY GROUND FORCES: IMKER-GRUPPE

Commanders
Comandante Pujales with a captain of the Nationalist Army Tank Battalion. (Ramiro Bujeiro)

Insignia
All members of *Gruppe Drohne* were given this badge to wear on the pocket of their tunics.

Flag
Flag of the Nationalist Army Tank Group.

The corresponding orders were placed through the company HISMA Ltda; the first on July 13, 1937 and the second on November 12, 1938.

The first order came straight from the General Headquarters of the *Generalísimo*, who urged *General* Sperrle to try to persuade Berlin to speed up the delivery of the thirty tanks requested together with other war materiel. The mediation of the head of the Legion Condor must have been decisive since on August 25 a shipment of eighteen Panzer I Ausf.A tanks arrived by sea at Ferrol. Five days later the other twelve tanks arrived in Seville,

Hauptmann Wolf
Right. The commander of the German 2nd Tank Company during a celebration at the unit's headquarters together with some of his men.

thus completing the order of thirty. All were sent to Cubas de la Sagra, where a company of sixteen tanks was formed. The rest were used to cover combat losses in other companies.

In the second order, made by *Major* Wilhelmi, German liaison officer between *Gruppe Imker* and the General Headquarters of the *Generalísimo*, "Twenty German tanks, some of which to be armed with cannon of 20mm or a larger caliber" were requested.

This request received a favorable response and on January 20, 1939, the tanks ordered were delivered to the Tank Groups, all type Ausf.A machines. The Germans sent no further armored materiel to Spain during the 1936-1939 civil war. Thus a total of 122 Panzerkampfwagen I were sent, of types A, B and command (Panzerbefehlswagen).

Tank crews
These strangely dressed men belonged to the *Gruppe Drohne* group of German instructors.

The Role Played by Ground Forces: Imker-Gruppe

Killed in combat
Plaque in memory of the German tank commander, Georg Scheuern, *Unteroffizier* of the General Staff of the *Panzergruppe Drohne*, killed in action on October 12, 1937 in Asturias.

Gruppe Thoma contributed a company of anti-tank guns to the tank unit for joint operations as support against enemy armored vehicles. This company was equipped with eight anti-tank guns, specifically 37mm Panzerabwehrkanone (PaK) 35/36, all with their own off-road Krupp L-2H43 "Protze" tow trucks; and another five guns to act independently which needed to be carried on trucks.

News
A group of members of *Panzergruppe Drohne* listening to a German radio station.

Instructions
Left. *Hauptmann* Wolf gives instructions to a Moroccan soldier.

Relax
Below, left. A member of the *Gruppe* writing at the end of a day's work.

Toy
A Panzer I like the one we can see in the photo above, but this time made of tinplate.

The Role Played by Ground Forces: Imker-Gruppe

Belt buckle
A belt buckle of a German uniform.

Hauptfeldwebel
A *Hauptfeldwebel* of Drohne Group wears the badge of his unit on his breast.

Formation
Above. German soldiers formed up in front of tanks.

Shooting practice
Hauptmann Wolf shooting a Luger pistol.

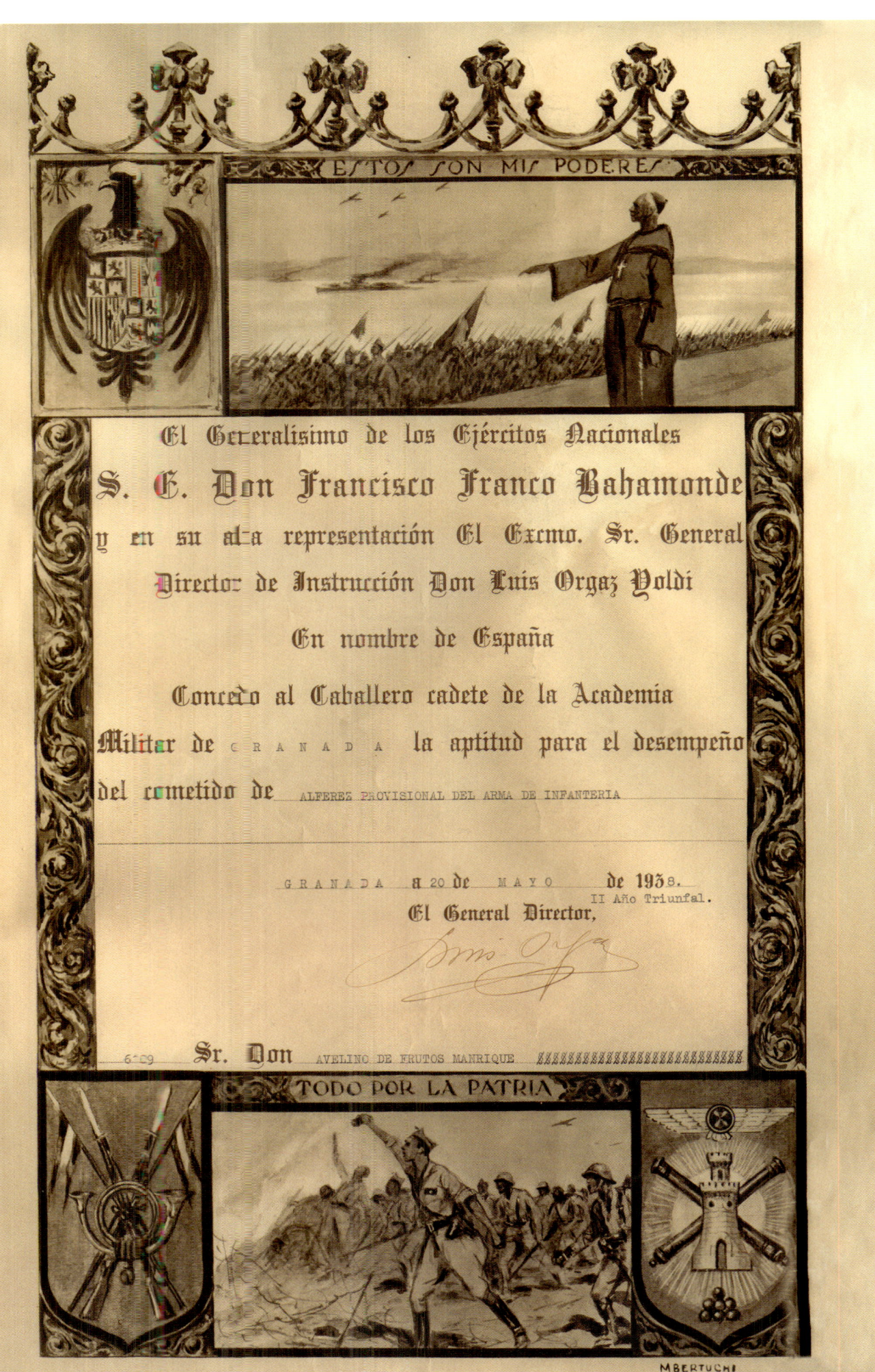

Instructors
A number of German instructors photographed with their Spanish trainees.

Wound badge
Above. Black wound badge in its original case.

Diploma
Previous page. Certificate of competence for the rank of *alférez provisional* (ensign) in the infantry.

Oath of allegiance
Below. Two images of an oath of allegiance ceremony, held in front of the ruins of the Simancas Barracks (Gijón), in which future provisional officers swear their allegiance.

2. IMKER AUSBILDER. TRAINERS AT THE NATIONAL ACADEMIES

Gruppe Issendorf

In mid-March 1937, the General Headquarters of the *Generalísimo* gave its go ahead for a team of German officers who had been serving in Spain for a month and half under *Oberstleutnant* Walter von Issendorff to provide their services as trainers to the *Milicias de Falange Española de las JONS* (Militias of the Spanish Phalanx of the Assemblies of the National Syndicalist Offensive).

These German officers had arrived in Spain between late January and early February of that same year to help with the military training of NCOs of the units of the militias organized by the Falangists to fight on the battle fronts.

German
Left. A German instructor at an *Academia de Provisionales* (Provisional Officers Academy).

Souvenir
Right. A number of Spanish trainees photographed with their German instructor.

The first *Academia de Jefes de Centuria de Falange* (Falangist Company Commander Academy) was set up on the "La Jarilla" estate in the province of Sevilla, where early in February some fifty Falangist party members began their training, with teachers from the *Primera Línea de FE de las JONS* (a Falangist militia organization) and German military instructors recently arrived in Spain. *Oberleutnant* Peter Bozung was the head of the instructors aided by Joachim von Knobloch (of the same rank) and another three recently arrived *Leutnants*.

At that same time, the Nationalist Militia Command decided to organize nine teams of instructors to train officers in nine different cities in provinces controlled by the insurgents. These teams and the staff organization would be made up of a total of forty-eight German officers and three assistants, many of them from the reserve. In April they would be joined by *Leutnant* Oskar Dirlewanger, a sinister character who years later, during the Second World War, would end up commanding a strange and atypical division of the Waffen-SS.

After the Decree of Unification in May 1937, all these academies were dissolved and the German staff was transferred to provisional officer and NCO training academies of the Spanish Army.

Jura
Below. Oath of allegiance of *sargentos provisionales* passing out from Vitoria Academy, June 26, 1937. To the right, a German infantry badge.

Orgaz
General Luis Orgaz Yoldi was appointed Head of the MIR (Mobilization Instruction and Recuperation) bureau by Franco. He was responsible for the *Academias de Provisionales* until the end of 1938 when he took command of the Levante Army.

The Transformation of the Gruppe Issendorff. The Academias de Provisionales

The structure of the provisional officer and NCO training academies (*Academias de Provisionales*), and the advanced training academies, meant that it was impossible to have enough fully active trainers and instructors, since the academies made use of retired, disabled or convalescent officers. This problem was particularly acute in infantry academies since there was the additional problem that this type of Spanish personnel were not able to conduct physical and field training exercises which required younger trainers with a high level of physical fitness.

This serious problem was resolved after a number of agreements were reached with the Germans stationed in Spain, by making use of "*negrillo*" tank instructors, using trainers from the now defunct Falangist schools, and complementing the staff with fresh German military trainers and monitors who had passed out from the former academies.

Spanish wine
Below, left. The German instructors fraternizing with the Spanish officers at one of the infantry academies.

Instructor
Below, right. A German *Leutnant* infantry instructor.

Visits
Above. Several German officer instructors visiting the ruins of some of the defenses of the Iron Belt of Bilbao.

In each of the infantry academies to which Germans were assigned, there was a Team Leader, normally an *Oberstleutnant*, although he might also be a *Major* or even a *Hauptmann*, a number of company commanders (*Hauptmann* or *Oberleutnant*) and section commanders (*Oberleutnant* or *Leutnant*), and a number of instructors, who were often *Oberfeldwebel* or *Feldwebel* rank.

Turnover was constant and there were very few cases of German trainers staying their whole time in Spain in the same academy.

Franco
The Germans took many souvenirs of Spain home with them, including this plaque with Franco's head on it.

German *Hauptfeldwebel*
Another photo of an oath of allegiance of *sargentos provisionales*. On this occasion the new NCOs are led by a *Hauptfeldwebel* of Panzergruppe Thoma.

THE ROLE PLAYED BY GROUND FORCES: IMKER-GRUPPE

Fellowship meal
After the oath of allegiance of *sargentos provisionales* passing out from Vitoria Academy, held on June 26, 1937.

Oath of allegiance
In the *Plaza Mayor* of Salamanca on March 18, 1938, corresponding to the 4th class of Avila of *alféreces provisionales*.

Shooting practice
Below, right. A German instructor practicing with a Mauser rifle at an *Academia de Provisionales*.

Other German Instructors

In addition to taking part in the training of Spanish tank crews and teaching in the infantry *Academias de Provisionales*, the Germans also trained Spanish troops in the use of other materiel and techniques, such as 37mm anti-tank guns, flamethrowers, tank transporting using heavy vehicles, Krupp L-H43 "Protze" light truck driving, maintenance, chemical warfare, artillery (*Gruppe Lucht*), 77mm mine launcher, driving, signals (*Gruppe Siber*), sappers-minelayers, and they even formed part of staff of teachers at the San Fernando Military Naval School until well into 1940. These latter teachers would be the last German instructors to leave Spain.

¡ARRIBA ESPAÑA!
¡VIVA FRANCO!

A Don Valentín Ochoa, Soldado

Como recuerdo al servicio militar en la
LEGION CONDOR ~ Grupo IMKER-HORCH ~
25.7.1938 — 20.5.1939
durante la guerra civil.

Torrejon de Velasco
AÑO de la VICTORIA

Comandante y Jefe del
Grupo IMKER-HORCH

The Role Played by Ground Forces: Imker-Gruppe

Radio
Germans of the Legion Condor using transmitters during operations.

3. Imker-Horch (Gruppe Wolm). Radio-Interception unit

Volunteer
A member of the *Gruppe Wolm* (according to his arm badge) photographing some corner of Spain.

One of the lesser-known units of the Legion Condor is the special radio-interception unit of the *Heer*, known as *Imker Horch-Kompanie*. Very little is known about this unit, since its participation in the Spanish civil war was cloaked in the utmost secrecy, both in terms of what it did and the reports it sent to the different units on a daily basis.

The interception unit, known in Spain as the *Gruppe Wolm*, operated in the areas of the fronts where there was most enemy activity and its main purpose was to intercept radio and telephony traffic to collect information about enemy troop deployment and chains of command. In particular the unit tried to discover where the Republicans were going to launch their offensives.

Flamenco
Some women in flamenco dresses and a flamenco guitarist entertain a German serving in the Radio-Interception Company.

The officers responsible for signals intelligence reported to "Ic." officers (who were the intelligence officers of general staffs and other staff units), who told them which sector or sectors they should pay special attention to. Most of the radio interception work aimed at intercepting traffic at the lower levels (battalion or regiment level), which was the easiest to decode, paying special attention to the signals networks of the Republican artillery and armored units. However, they also maintained close surveillance over

Organizational Chart of the Gruppe Imker

MANDO GRUPPE IMKER
Oberstleutnant H. Freiher von Funck

PLANA MAYOR IMKER

- **GRUPPE THOMA** — Oberstleutnan: W.von Thoma
  - **PLANA MAYOR G. THOMA** — Major E. von Ostmann
    - **1ª COMPAÑÍA PANZER** — Oberleutnant J. Ziegler
    - **2ª COMPAÑÍA PANZER** — Oberleutnant H. Wolf
    - **3ª COMPAÑÍA PANZER** — Hauptmann K.E. Bothe
  - **TALLER** — Oberleutnant A. Schneider
  - **COMPAÑÍA DE TRANSPORTE** — Oberleutnant H. Schruefer
  - **INSTRUCCIÓN ANTITANQUE** — Hauptmann P. Jansa
  - **INSTRUCCIÓN LANZALLAMAS**
  - **ARMERÍA**

- **GRUPPE WOLM** — Oberleutnant Hertzer
  - **STAB GRUPPE WOLM**
    - 1ª SECCIÓN
    - 2ª SECCIÓN
    - 3ª SECCIÓN

El *Imker Ausbilder* dependía de von Thoma. En septiembre de 1938 se fusionó con el *Gruppe Thoma*.

signals from brigades and divisions of the Popular Army, as well as other military establishments, such as the Republican fleet, the air raid warning system, and the general headquarters of the Popular Republican Army.

The *Horch-Kompanie* operating in Spain was commanded by a *Hauptmann* and was divided into three sections, each led by a *Leutnant*, who acted independently at various locations within Nationalist territory.

Each section had the necessary resources to capture enemy information; they had specialists in the interception of long wave, short wave, telephony and even telegraphy signals.

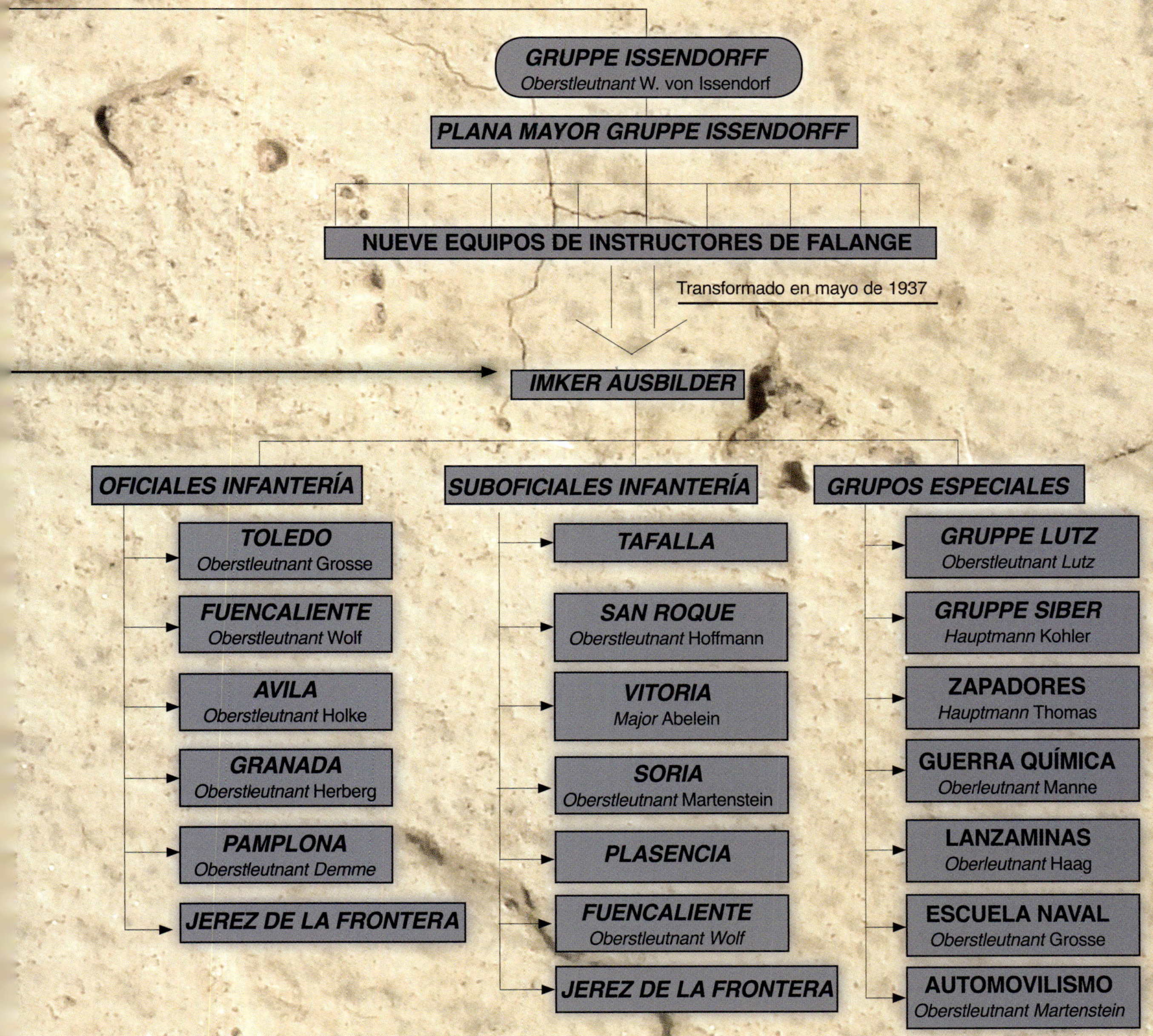

Sergeant
A *Feldwebel* of the Imker-Horch Group with a Spanish woman.

GRUPPE ISSENDORFF
Oberstleutnant W. von Issendorf

PLANA MAYOR GRUPPE ISSENDORFF

NUEVE EQUIPOS DE INSTRUCTORES DE FALANGE

Transformado en mayo de 1937

IMKER AUSBILDER

OFICIALES INFANTERÍA

- **TOLEDO** — *Oberstleutnant* Grosse
- **FUENCALIENTE** — *Oberstleutnant* Wolf
- **AVILA** — *Oberstleutnant* Holke
- **GRANADA** — *Oberstleutnant* Herberg
- **PAMPLONA** — *Oberstleutnant* Demme
- **JEREZ DE LA FRONTERA**

SUBOFICIALES INFANTERÍA

- **TAFALLA**
- **SAN ROQUE** — *Oberstleutnant* Hoffmann
- **VITORIA** — *Major* Abelein
- **SORIA** — *Oberstleutnant* Martenstein
- **PLASENCIA**
- **FUENCALIENTE** — *Oberstleutnant* Wolf
- **JEREZ DE LA FRONTERA**

GRUPOS ESPECIALES

- **GRUPPE LUTZ** — *Oberstleutnant* Lutz
- **GRUPPE SIBER** — *Hauptmann* Kohler
- **ZAPADORES** — *Hauptmann* Thomas
- **GUERRA QUÍMICA** — *Oberleutnant* Manne
- **LANZAMINAS** — *Oberleutnant* Haag
- **ESCUELA NAVAL** — *Oberstleutnant* Grosse
- **AUTOMOVILISMO** — *Oberstleutnant* Martenstein

CHAPTER IV

IV

The Role Played by the Navy

Deutschland
Pocket battleship *Deutschland*, one of three vessels of this class built by Germany, which took part in the Spanish Civil War.

Uniform
Jacket and cap of a German sailor.

In addition to the role played by the air and ground services of the German armed forces in the Spanish conflict, which we have already dealt with in previous chapters, the navy also contributed their grain of sand to the victory of the Nationalist forces. While in terms of the number of men involved and the amount of materiel deployed the German navy's contribution cannot compare to the part played by the *Luftwaffe* or the *Heer*, its role was of great importance in the arena of naval warfare.

After the creation of Special Staff W (*Sonderstab W*) late in July 1936 in order to plan the delivery and organization of German aid to the insurgent forces in Spain, a special naval section was set up within *Sonderstab W* which was known as the *Schiffahrtabteilung* (Shipping Department), which would be responsible for all matters relating to sea traffic to the Spanish mainland. This was initially the mission entrusted to the naval units attached to the *Schiffahrtabteilung*, but the reality was that in a few months those units became an active part the war itself, with surface and submarine vessels being involved in various naval incidents.

Sailor
Two photos of a German *matrose* (seaman) who took part in the Spanish Civil War.

Paperweight
A three-gun turret of a pocket battleship.

The first mission that vessels of the *Kriegsmarine* took part in was to protect German merchantmen ferrying military materiel to the ports of Nationalist Spain. Later they also provided every possible maritime support to the understrength Nationalist Navy, while Germany navy personnel helped train Spanish crews. The first commander of the collection of *Kriegsmarine* vessels ordered by high command to serve in Spanish waters was *Konteradmiral* Rolf Carls.

Admiral Scheer
The three modern German pocket battleships patrolled the Spanish coast during the war.

Torpedo boat
The *See Adler* was a *Rabvogel*-class *torpedoboot* that patrolled Spanish waters.

In August 1936 a small naval contingent arrived in Spain comprising three officers and ten specialists in mines, radio-communications and coastal artillery. It was led by *Kapitän zur See* Kurt Meyer-Döhner, German navy representative in the Nationalist zone who throughout the war would be responsible for all German naval aid to Franco's Spain.

At each of the ports at which war materiel from Germany was disembarked (mainly El Ferrol, Vigo, and Cadiz, and in the first months of the war, also Lisbon) German naval officers were appointed to oversee and supervise the shipments. The officer stationed at El Ferrol also had twelve German technicians under him with various duties related to marine warfare, among which were the assembly of communications, naval firing control systems, and anti-aircraft cannon and machine guns on a number of vessels of the Nationalist Navy, not to mention the organization of the Cantabrian minesweeping fleet.

Commander
Konteradmiral Rolf Carls was one of the commanders of the German navy serving in Spanish waters during the conflict.

Leipzig
8,000-ton light cruiser launched in 1931. It made three patrols in Spanish waters during the conflict.

Raubtier class
Bow-on view of one of the *Raubtier*-class torpedo boats, probably the last of the series: the *Tiger*.

In memoriam
Below, right. A simple monument in memory of the victims of the bombing of the pocket battleship *Deutschland* off the coast of Ibiza.

After the official formation of the Legion Condor in November 1936, a new naval contingent, this time more numerous, was sent to Spain, designated *Gruppe Nordsee*. Ten officers and seventy specialists under the command of *Korvettenkapitän* Schottky arrived with the task of training Spanish seamen in naval communications, coastal defense, mines and in the use of torpedoes, as well as modern naval strategy and tactics. They set up their bases at El Ferrol, Palma de Mallorca and Cadiz.

In addition to these advisers and technicians, the sea transport group also grew. This group, which was based in Vigo, was in charge of supplying the Legion Condor's ground and air units.

Towards the end of the war, twenty-eight naval instructors remained in Spain (three officers and twenty-five NCOs), as well as six civilian translators.

Cruiser
Contemporary painting representing a *Leipzig* class cruiser at full steam.

The total cost of the materiel supplied by the *Kriegsmarine* amounted to 2,674,647.19 Reichmarks.

With regard to the German naval involvement in Spanish waters, perhaps the best remembered event was the bombing by Republican twin-engined Tupolev SB-2 *Katiuskas* of the pocket battleship *Deutschland* on May 29, 1937. This ship formed part of the Naval Non-Intervention Patrol and was

Deutschland
A spectacular photo of the battleship *Deutschland*, with a dedication by *Vizeadmiral* Marschall written just after the end of the war, in Malaga.

U-Boote
One of the German submarines which patrolled Spanish waters during the Civil War.

at anchor close to, albeit outside, the port of Ibiza, alongside the torpedo boat *Leopard* and the tanker *Neptun*. The German ship was hit by two 250kg bombs, while another fell to one side, sinking the captain's launch. Apart from the material damage caused, twenty-two sailors were killed instantly and several more were injured, of which nine subsequently died.

As a reprisal for this attack, the pocket battleship *Admiral Scheer* received orders from Berlin to bombard the city of Almeria. The attack was carried out on May 31, just two days later.

With regard to the war beneath the waves, one significant event that remained for many years clouded in a mist of ignorance, if not mystery, was the operation known by German high command as "Operation Ursula." This was planned as a series of training maneuvers for the crews of submarines U-33 and U-34, commanded by *Kapitän zur See* Kurt Freiwald and *Kapitän zur See* Harald Grosse, respectively, but the secret mission was to attack any Republican warships they might encounter.

Bombing of Almeria
As a reprisal for the Republican bombing of the *Deutschland*, the Kriegsmarine planned the naval bombing of Almeria, carried out by the *Admiral Scheer* on May 31, 1937.

THE ROLE PLAYED BY THE NAVY

Artillery
Three-gun forward turret, fitted with 280mm guns, on the pocket battleship *Deutschland*. Also in the photo are the caskets of the crewmembers who perished in the bombing raid by the Republican air force.

Military honors
The funeral for the victims of the *Deutschland* took place in the British colony of Gibraltar, with military honors rendered by the Royal Navy.

LEGION CONDOR

Documentation
Spanish military ID belonging to *Oberfeldwebel* Alfred Nordbeck, attached to the Navy General Staff.

On December 1, 1936 the two submarines started to patrol the waters between the Cabo de Palos and the Cabo del Nao in the case of the former, and from the west of the Cabo of Palos to Cartagena the latter. Ten days later, without having achieved anything whatsoever, they took their leave of these waters and headed once again for Germany.

However, on its return journey, U-34 encountered the Republican submarine C-3 just outside the city of Malaga. It launched a torpedo and sank the enemy vessel without being detected. This was the only victory scored on this mission.

THE ROLE PLAYED BY THE NAVY

Seaplane
Previous page, below. Remains of the Heinkel He 60 seaplane carried by the pocket battleship *Deutschland* after the Republican bombing.

German Vessels Patrolling Spanish Waters Throughout the War

* Pocket battleships:	*Deutschland*, *Admiral Scheer* and *Admiral Graf Spee*
* Cruisers:	*Emden*, *Königsberg*, *Köln*, *Nürnberg* and *Leipzig*.
* Torpedo boats:	*Leopard*, *Albatros*, *Seeadler*, *Falke*, *Greif*, *Jaguar*, *Iltis*, *Kondor*, *Luchs*, *Möwe*, *Tiger* and *Wolf*.
* Submarines:	U-33 and U-34 (operating in the Mediterranean), plus U-14, U-19, U-25, U-26, U-27, U-28, U-29, U-30, U-31, U-32, U-35 and U-36.

Signalman
Naval signalman on a vessel of the Kriegsmarine.

The naval contingent was led at various times and for various periods by the *Konteradmirals* Rolf Carls (who commanded Spanish waters for more than one period), Hermann Boehm, Hermann von Fischel, Wilhelm Marschall, and Paul Wenneker.

Torpedoboot
Tiger torpedo boat

CHAPTER V

Die Legions-Kapelle bringt uns eine Abwechslung!

V

Miscellaneous

1. The Materiel Used

Klemm 32 A XIV light aircraft

Messerschmitt Bf 108

Air Materiel

Arado Ar 68 E	Biplane fighter
Arado Ar 95 W	Reconnaissance and attack seaplane
Dornier Do 17 E, F and P	Twin-engined reconnaissance and bomber
Fieseler Fi 156 A	Light personnel transport
Heinkel He 45 B	Reconnaissance and light bomber biplane
Heinkel He 46 C	Reconnaissance and support
Heinkel He 50 G	Ground-attack biplane
Heinkel He 51 B	Biplane fighter
Heinkel He 59 B	Reconnaissance and attack seaplane
Heinkel He 60 E	Reconnaissance and light bomber seaplane
Heinkel He 70 E and F	Reconnaissance and light bomber

Air Materiel

Heinkel He 111 B and E	Bomber
Heinkel He 112 V	Ground-attack fighter, prototype
Henschel Hs 123 A	Dive-bomber biplane
Henschel Hs 126 A	Reconnaissance and support
Junkers Ju 52/3mg3e	Transport and bomber
Junkers Ju 52/3mg4e	Transport and bomber, marine version
Junkers Ju 86 D	Bomber
Junkers Ju 87 A and B	Dive bomber
Junkers W 34 hi	Liaison, bomber and trainer
Klemm 32 a XIV	Personnel transport
Messerschmitt Bf 108 B	Light transport and liaison
Messerschmitt Bf 109 B, C, D and E	Fighter

According to official data, the total number of aircraft sent by Germany to equip the Legion Condor was 600. However, in addition to the aircraft listed, during the war Germany supplied the Nationalist Air Force with other types of aircraft which were not used by the German unit.

MISCELLANEOUS

Ground Materiel

Panzerkampfwagen I (Sd.Kfz 101) Ausf.A	Light tank
Panzerkampfwagen I (Sd.Kfz 101) Ausf.B	Light tank
Panzerbefehlswagen I (Sd.Kfz 163) Ausf.B	Light command tank
Panzerkampfwagen I (Sd.Kfz 101) Ausf.A "Ohne Aufbau"	Trainer tank for drivers (no turret and open)
Flak 30	Light anti-aircraft cannon (machine gun)
Flak 18 mod. 1935	Light anti-aircraft cannon
Flak 18 (85/56)	Heavy anti-aircraft cannon
PaK 35/36 mod. 1933	Anti-tank guns

245

As mentioned in the note to the previous list, the Reich also supplied the Nationalist Army with other types of artillery pieces that were not used by the Legion Condor.

Other Ground Materiel

SdKfz 7 mittlerer Zugkraftwagen	Half-track used to tow artillery pieces
Henschel-Diesel 33 D1/G1	Medium off-road truck (there were also models with van-type bodywork -Kfz. 61 /Kfz. 62-)
Mercedes-Benz G3a (6x4)	Truck
Mercedes-Benz LG63/LG 3000 (6x4)	Truck (there were also a bowser version for the air force: Kfz. 384)
Büssing-NAG Type G31 (Kfz. 61)	Truck
Büssing-NAG 80	Truck
Krupp L2H-43 "Protze" (Kfz. 69 and Kfz. 70)	Truck
Krupp L3 5M242 (Kfz. 42)	Truck
Krupp L3H-163 (Kfz. 62/63)	Truck (also used as a signals vehicle)
MAN Z 1	Truck
Vomag DL.48	Truck
MAN E.3000	Truck and bus
Opel Blitz mod. 1935 of 2 MT, 2.5 MT, and 3 MT (Kfz. 31)	Truck (the 2.5 MT version was also used as an ambulance)
Phänomen Granit. 2500H (Kfz. 31)	Ambulance
Auto-Unión (Kfz. 31)	Ambulance
4x4 Type 40, on Auto-Unión/Horch 901 chassis (Kfz. 15)	Medium vehicle

MISCELLANEOUS

Other Ground Materiel

Mercedes-Benz 170V 4x2 (Kfz. 2)	Light command and liaison vehicle
Auto-Unión KG/Horch 830 R (Kfz. 12 and Kfz. 15)	Light vehicle
Hanomag Garant Kfz. 4/20	Medium vehicle
Mercedes-Benz 320 Wk 4x2 (Kfz. 12)	Light vehicle
Mercedes-Benz 230 Berlina	Light vehicle
Mercedes-Benz MB-770	Official armored light vehicle
Mercedes 540-K Berlina	Drop-top light vehicle
Wanderer W-11 4x2 (Kfz. 12)	Light vehicle
Horch 951 Sedan	Light vehicle
Sd.Ah.42	Signals trailer
Sd.Ah.115	Flat-bed tank trailer
DKW NZ-350	Motorcycle (with and without sidecar)
BMW R-12	Motorcycle (with and without sidecar)
BMW R-35	Motorcycle
Zündapp KS 600	Motorcycle
Zündapp K 800	Motorcycle

Hugo Sperrle
First commander of the Legion Condor.

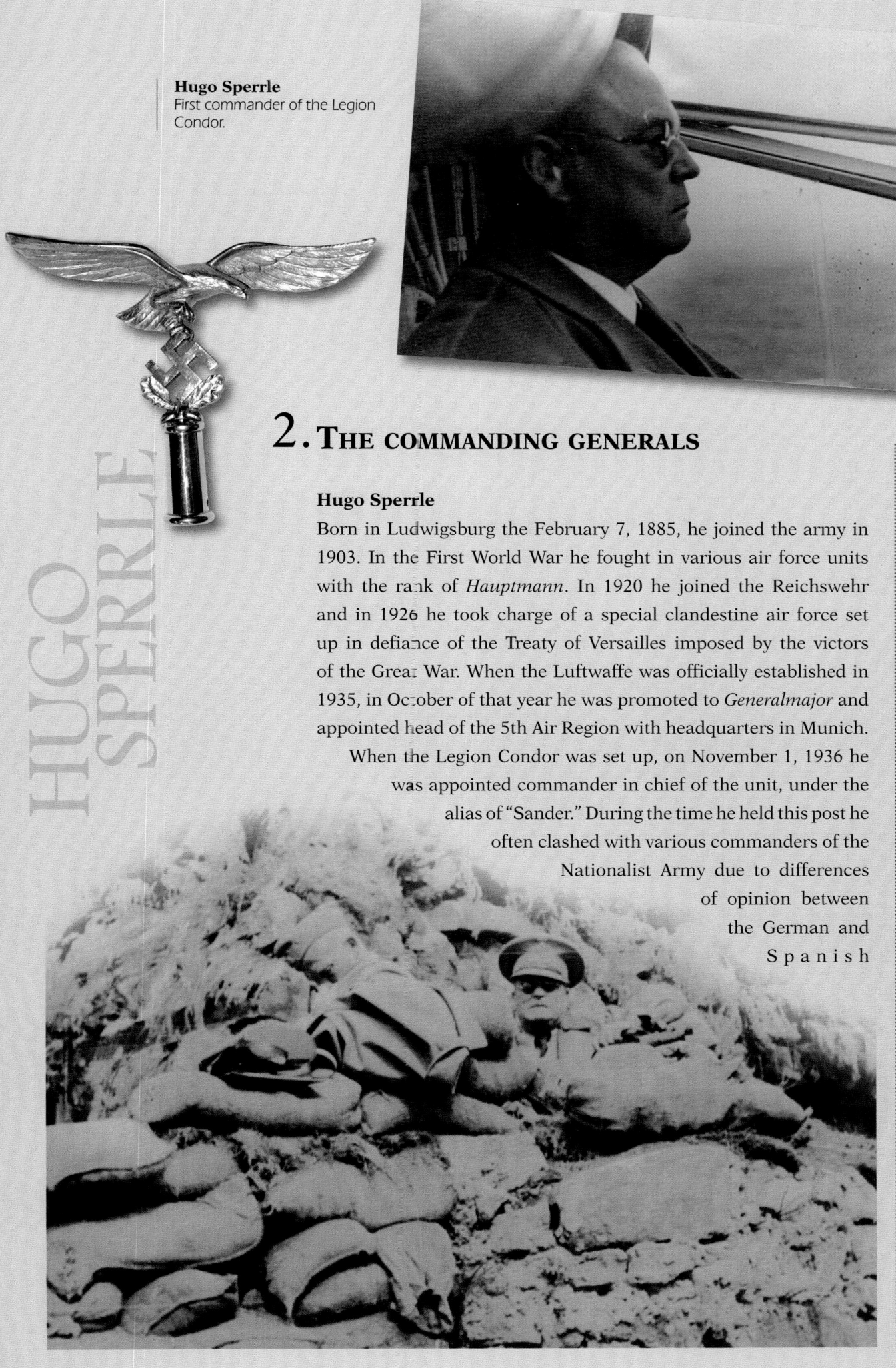

2. THE COMMANDING GENERALS

Hugo Sperrle

Born in Ludwigsburg the February 7, 1885, he joined the army in 1903. In the First World War he fought in various air force units with the rank of *Hauptmann*. In 1920 he joined the Reichswehr and in 1926 he took charge of a special clandestine air force set up in defiance of the Treaty of Versailles imposed by the victors of the Great War. When the Luftwaffe was officially established in 1935, in October of that year he was promoted to *Generalmajor* and appointed head of the 5th Air Region with headquarters in Munich.

When the Legion Condor was set up, on November 1, 1936 he was appointed commander in chief of the unit, under the alias of "Sander." During the time he held this post he often clashed with various commanders of the Nationalist Army due to differences of opinion between the German and Spanish military establishments as to how the war should conducted. It was during this period that the bombing of the Basque town of Guernica occurred and some historians place the responsibility for that operation at his door. On October 31, 1937, he bade farewell to the *Generalísimo* at Burgos after having been relieved the previous day by *General* Volkmann. Shortly afterwards he returned to Germany.

In January 1939 he took command of the 3rd *Luftflotte*, one of the three Air Fleets into which the Luftwaffe was divided. During the Western campaign in 1940, he continued at the head of that Air Fleet, which was deployed in France at the end of that campaign. In July of that year he was promoted to field marshal, responsible for the air forces over the Western front until August 1944, when he was relieved from his post and replaced by *General* Dessloch. He then moved on to the Luftwaffe High Command and later the Luftwaffe Supreme Command.

After the end of the war he was arrested by the victorious army in the south of Germany in May 1945 and brought to trial in Nüremberg in 1948, where he was cleared of all the charges brought against him. He died on April 2, 1953 in Munich, after an operation on his stomach.

Conversation
Sperrle converses with General Franco on the Northern front.

Lookout point
Below. General Sperrle with his Chief of Staff, the then *Oberst* von Richthofen, during the operations against Vizcaya.

HELMUTH VOLKMANN

Helmuth Volkmann
He took over command of the Legion Condor from Sperrle. In the photo he is with Spanish air chief, *General* Alfredo Kindelán.

Helmuth Volkmann

Helmuth Volkmann was one of the lesser-known German officers of the first half of the 20th century and his career was one of the more mysterious. Born on February 28, 1889 in Diedenhofen, he joined the armed forces in 1907. He fought in the First World War as an army officer and once the war was over he held a number of different posts in the new Reichswehr until in September 1934 he entered the Luftwaffe, by which time he had reached the rank of *Oberst*. Between June 1936 and October 1937 he headed the Air Force Administration Department, now as a *Generalmajor*. While occupying this post he encountered some friction with *Generals* Göring and Milch with regard to the financial restrictions that had to be applied to arming the Luftwaffe.

On November 1, 1937 he replaced *General* Sperrle as commander in chief of the Legion Condor, an organization he led, under the pseudonym "*Veith,*" until the end of October 1938. By this time he held the rank of *Generalleutnant*,

General Staff
Volkmann and Kindelán with members of their general staff.

officially bestowed on him on April 1, 1938, although he was an acting *Generalleutnant* from the moment he took command of the Condor.

His replacement was *Generalmajor* Wolfram *Fr.* von Richthofen

His stay in Spain was characterized by his major discrepancies with the strategy of the Nationalist high command in the planning and execution of military operations. He also, albeit unsuccessfully, tried to persuade Berlin to significantly increase the power of the unit under his command.

On his return to Germany he held high-ranking posts in the Air Ministry between November 1938 and March 1939, by which time he had risen to the rank of *General der Flieger*. On the following April 1 he took charge of the Luftwaffe's Air War Academy, where he trained officers of the air force general staff and senior officers destined to rise to the rank of general. He continued in this role until the following September, when he was made commander of the 94th Infanterie-Division, following his promotion on August 25 to *General der Infanterie*. He led that unit on the Western front, until on August 4, 1940 he was involved in a car accident. Seventeen days later he died at the Berlin-Gatow Hospital as a result of the injuries he sustained.

Visit to La Cenia
Above and below. *General* Kindelán visiting the head of the Legion Condor at La Cenia airfield (Tarragona). In the foreground of both photos, Volkmann's interpreter, *Major* Max Buch.

WOLFRAM FREIHERR VON RICHTHOFEN

***Generalmajor* von Richthofen**
Third and final commander of the Legion Condor, he took over from Volkmann. In the photo, von Richthofen during the Second World War, with *Generalfeldmarschall* Milch.

Wolfram *Freiherr* von Richthofen

This officer, held by many to be one of the most outstanding senior officers both technically and tactically, was born in Gut Barzdorf, Striegau, Silesia, on October 10, 1895. He pursued his military education at the Gross-Lichterfelde Academy and fought in the First World War with the rank of *leutnant* in the 4th "*von Schill*" Hussar Regiment on the eastern and western fronts. In 1917 he joined the air force and by the end of that year he was flying with the legendary "*Richthofen*" fighter squadron in which his cousins Manfred, the famous Red Baron, and Lothar also flew.

In 1920 he retired from the air force to start his university education at Hannover where he studied mechanical engineering. Three years later he rejoined the Reichswehr, since the economic situation in Germany at that time made civilian jobs hard to find. However, he was able to continue with his studies and graduated as a Diploma Engineer in May 1924 before receiving his doctorate in engineering in 1929. In 1925, like many other former – and new – pilots, he was sent to Lipetsk, a secret training center in Soviet Russia.

Between 1929 and 1932 he held the post of air attaché in Rome, where he became friends with Marshal Italo Balbo, one of the pioneers of Italian aviation. On returning to Germany he held a number of posts, including a job in the planning department of the Air Ministry and the top management position at the Rechlin Test Center from 1934 a 1935.

Legion Condor

Late in 1936 he was made Chief of the general Staff of the Legion Condor in Spain, a position he took up in January of the following year. In this role he excelled as an organizer of the use of the air force in combat against the Republican air force and against enemy targets on the ground (his work was especially important during the Northern campaign between March and October 1937, in which he was Chief of Staff of the entire Nationalist Air Force – the Spanish, Italian and German air forces – in that sector of operations).

Relieved along with his superior *General* Sperrle, at the end of October 1937, he took command, now back in Germany, of *Kampfgeschwader* 257 (Bomber Wing 257).

Now with the rank of *Generalmajor*, on November 1, 1938 he returned to Spain, but this time as commander in chief of the Legion Condor, a post he held until the end of the conflict. He was awarded the Spanish Cross in Gold with Swords and Diamonds and the Spanish *Medalla Militar Individual* in a special version with diamonds (like his two unit commanders before him).

On returning to Germany for a brief period he held the post of *Fliegerführer z.b.V.* (Special Purpose Air Command) in Berlin and commanded the *Flieger-Division z.b.V.* This latter post he held for just a couple of days before taking command of the 8th Air Corps at the end of the Polish campaign. At the head of this great unit he would take part in the campaigns of France, the Balkans, the Mediterranean and the Soviet Union. These successes earned him his promotion, on February 1, 1942, to *Generaloberst* and the command of *Luftflotte* 4 early in July.

Reviewing the troops
Generalmajor von Richthofen reviews a *Luftwaffe* unit accompanied by Hermann Göring. He wears the Spanish Cross on his breast.

Zaragoza
Below. Air parade at Sanjurjo airfield. Von Richthofen reviews his men.

MISCELLANEOUS

Next to Milch
Above. Von Richthofen, commander of the VIII Air Corps, next to the "number two" of the Luftwaffe.

García Morato
Right. Von Richthofen gives his condolences to *Comandante* García Morato's widow.

In 1940 he renewed his relationship with Spain. In September he was sent to have talks with Franco regarding Operation "Felix" (the capture of Gibraltar) as part of which operation von Richthofen would be responsible for the air forces involved.

On February 16, 1943 he became the youngest marshal of the German air force, and four months later he took command of *Luftflotte* 2 in Italy. At the end of October of the following year he resigned from that post, having been diagnosed with a brain tumor that was operated on that month.

Once he had received the all clear, from November 28, 1944 to May 1945 he occupied a post in the Luftwaffe high command. At the end of the war he was taken prisoner by a U.S. patrol in Bavaria, before dying in the Austrian town of Bad Ischl on July 12, 1945 as a result of a brain hemorrhage brought on by the tumor. He was buried in the military cemetery of that town. He had received the Knight's Cross on May 17, 1940 and Oak Leaves to the Knight's Cross on July 17, 1941.

Tribute
Generalmajor von Richthofen and his chief of staff, *Oberst* Seidemann, present a floral tribute in posthumous recognition of the hero, Joaquín García Morato.

Werner Mölders
With him, *General* Vigón and *Obersts* Plocher and Seidemann.

3. Aces of the Legion Condor

The Principal Air Aces and their Confirmed Victories

Air aces	Rank / unit	Number of kills
Mölders, Werner	*Hauptmann* - *Major* 3.J/88	14 (2 I-15, 11 I-16 and 1 SB-2 -plus 1 unconfirmed I-16)
Schellmann, Wolfgang	*Hauptmann* - *Major* 1.J/88	12 (2 I-15, 8 I-16 and 2 SB-2)
Harder, Harro	*Hauptmann* - *Major*	8 I-16)
Ensslen, Wilhelm	*Oberleutnant* / 2.J/88	9 (3 I-15, 5 I-16 and 1 SB-2)
Ihlefeld, Herbert	*Leutnant* / 2.J/88	9 (4 I-15, 4 I-16 and 1 SB-2)
Oesau, Walter	*Oberleutnant* / Ayte. J/88	9 (4 I-15, 4 I-16 and 1 SB-2)
Seiler, Reinhard	*Leutnant* / 2.J/88	9 (3 I-15, 2 I-16 and 4 SB-2)

MISCELLANEOUS

The Principal Air Aces and their Confirmed Victories

Air aces	Rank / unit	Number of kills
Knüppel, Herwig	*Hauptmann* / 4.J/88 - VJ/88	8 (1 Breguet XIX, 2 Potez, 3 Nieuport 46, 1 I-15 and 1 SB-2)
Mayer, Hans-Karl	*Oberleutnant* / 1.J/88	8 (1 I-15, 4 I-16 and 3 SB-2)
Balthasar, Wilhelm	*Oberleutnant* / 1 J/88 - 2.J/88	7 (3 I-16 and 4 SB-2)
Eberhardt, Kraft	*Oberleutnant* / Major 4.J/88	7 (2 Breguet XIX, 4 Potez and 1 I-15)
Grabmann, Walter	*Hauptmann* / Major J/88	7 (2 I-15, 3 I-16 and 2 SB-2)
Tietzen, Horst	*Leutnant* / 3.J/88 - 1.J/88	7 (7 I-16)
Pingel, Rolf	*Leutnant* / VJ/83 - 2.J/88	6 (1 I-15, 3 I-16 and 2 SB-2)
Rochel, Kurt	*Unteroffizier* / 2.J/88	6 (1 I-15 and 5 I-16)
Schob, Herbert	*Unteroffizier* / 2.J/88	6 (1 I-15 4 I-16 and 1 SB-2)

Walther Oesau

Rolf Pingel

LEGION CONDOR

Swastika
Photo below. At the Guzmanes de Leon Palace this "parasol" in the form of a swastika was set up in the inner courtyard.

Arches in Leon
This and following page. In the main streets of Leon triumphal arches were erected in honor of the Germans and to bid them farewell.

Die Deutsche Arbeitsfront

E.S. »ROBERT LEY«

Seereisen der

N.S.-Gemeinschaft »Kraft durch Freude«

M.S. Wilhelm Gustloff

M. S. „Wilhelm Gustloff"
Theatersaal

M. S. „Wilhelm Gustloff"
Hintere Halle

M. S. „Wilhelm Gustloff"
Große Halle

Wilhelm Gustloff
It was one of the vessels involved in repatriating the Legion Condor.

Vigo dock
Formation of German Legionnaires before embarking in Vigo bound for Hamburg.

Back to Germany
The Legion Condor returned to Germany on five vessels belonging to the organization "Strength through Joy" (*KdF*).

Parade in Hamburg
After disembarking in Hamburg, and after the troops were reviewed by Air Marshal Göring, the Legion Condor marched through the streets of the German port city.

Doberitz

At the Doberitz training ground, near Spandau (Berlin), a huge camp was set up to organize the victory parade in the capital city of the Reich. These two pages show different details of the camp and the review and march past presided over by Air Marshal Hermann Göring.

Berlin

On June 6, 1939 the Spanish War Victory Parade took place in Berlin. The event was presided over by Chancellor Adolf Hitler. That same day tribute was paid to all Legion Condor members who lost their lives in the armed conflict.
The stands for the event were set up in the *Berlinerstrasse*, opposite the *Techische Hochschule*.
In the lowermost photo of the next page, the first from the right is the Paymaster Colonel of the Spanish air force, Prince Alfonso de Orleans y Borbón.

MISCELLANEOUS

Parade and march-past
Photos of the parade and march-past held in Berlin to celebrate the homecoming of the Legion Condor.

Salute
Left. Chancellor Hitler salutes Spanish General Jose Solchaga, to whom he has just awarded the Order of the German Eagle. Behind we see Italian and Japanese military dignitaries.

Film
Below. Still from a contemporary film about the Legion Condor's parade in Berlin.

Legionnaires
This and subsequent pages. Collection of photos of German combatants in the Spanish Civil War (1936-1939).

MISCELLANEOUS

Publications
A large number of books were published in Germany when the volunteers of the Legion Condor returned. Here we can see a sample of the front covers of such books.

MISCELLANEOUS

Legion Condor

MISCELLANEOUS

Standard
During the Leon parade, held at La Virgen del Camino shortly before the Madrid Victory Parade, the Legion Condor was presented with a splendid standard to take back to their homeland and so maintain the tradition and memory of their participation in the war.
On the previous page we can admire a bronze figurine of the standard bearer made in Germany shortly after the Legion Condor's return.

Rings
An extraordinary collection of rings belonging to members of the Legion Condor. Most of them were engraved by their owners with the dates of their sojourn in Spain.

Legion Condor

MISCELLANEOUS

War souvenirs
In the following pages we can see objects made in Spain of all shapes and sizes that the German legionnaires took back to Germany with them.

MISCELLANEOUS

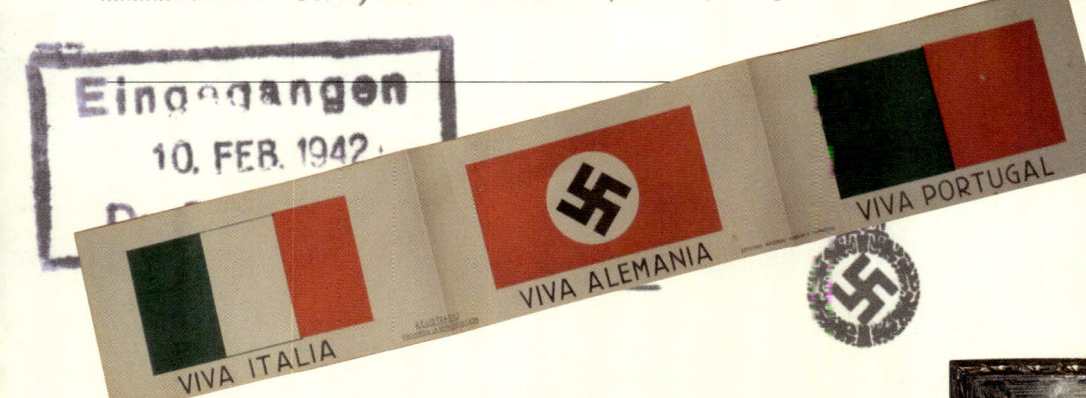

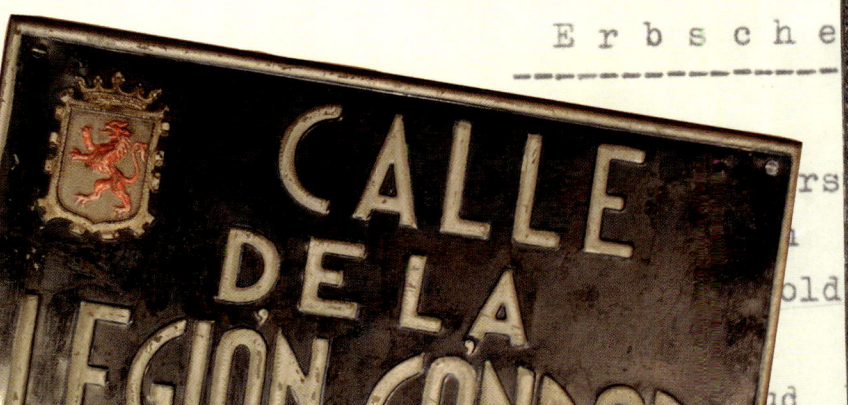

Plaque
Above. In the city of Leon the City Council dedicated street to the Legion Condor in memory of their stay there.

Strongbox
Used by the Legion Condor air corps.

Souvenir
Section of a piston of an aero-engine decorated by a German legionnaire as a souvenir of his stay in Spain.

Camera
Used by a member of the Legion Condor during the Spanish Civil War.

Objects
Various objects of the period among which we would highlight the wound badge (back and front) awarded to members of the Legion Condor who for one reason or another had been injured during the Spanish Civil War.

Bibliography

ABENDROTH, Hans-Henning: *Hitler in der Spanischen Arena: Die deutsch-spanischen beziehungen im Spannungsfeld der Europäischen Interessenpolitik von Ausbruch des Bürgerkrieges bis zum Ausbruch des Weltkrieges 1936-1939*, 1973.

ARIAS RAMOS, Raúl: *Legión Cóndor. Su historia 60 años después*, 2000.

ARIAS RAMOS, Raúl: *La Legión Cóndor. Imágenes inéditas para su historia*, 2002.

ARIAS RAMOS, Raúl: *La Legión Cóndor en la Guerra Civil. El apoyo militar alemán a Franco*, 2003.

ARIAS RAMOS, Raúl: *La Kriegsmarine en la Guerra Civil española*, 2005.

ARRÁEZ CERDÁ, Juan: *Los cazadores de la Legión Cóndor*, 1993.

BENDER, Roger James: *Legion Condor. Uniforms, Organization and History*, 1992.

BEUMELBURG, Werner: *Kampf um Spanien. Die Geschichte der Legion Condor*, 1939.

BLEY, Wulf, dir.: *Das Buch der Spanienflieger. Die Feuertaufe der neuen deutschen Luftwaffe*, 1939.

BUSCH, Fritz-Otto: *Kampf vor Spaniens Küsten. Deutsche Marine im Spanischen Bürgerkrieg*, 1939.

DRUMM, Karl: *Die deutsche Luftwaffe im Spanischen Bürgerkrieg (Legion Condor)*, 1957.

ELSTOB, Peter: *La Legión Cóndor. España 1936-39*, 1974.

FÜHRING, Hellmut-Hermann: *Wir funken für Franco. Einer von der Legion Erzahlt*, 1939.

GARRIGA ALEMANY, Ramón: *La Legión Cóndor*, 1975.

HIELCHER, Kurt: *Wir von der LN 88*, 1938.

HIDALGO SALAZAR, Ramón: *La ayuda alemana a España, 1936-1939*, 1975.

HOYOS, Max Graf: *Pedros y Pablos. Fliegen - Erleben - Kämpfen in Spanien*, 1940.

KOHL, Hermann: *Deutsche Flieger über Spanien*, 1939.

LAUREAU, Patrick and FERNÁNDEZ, José: *La Legion Condor*, 1999.

LENT, Alfred: *Wir kämpften für Spanien*, 1939.

MAIER, Klaus A.: *Guernica 26-4-1937. La intervención alemana en España y el caso Guernica*, 1976.

MERKES, Manfred *Die deutsche Politik gegenüber dem Spanischen Bürgerkrieg 1936-1939*, 1969.

MOLINA FRANCO, Lucas: *El legado de Sigfrido. La ayuda militar alemana al Ejército y la Marina nacional en la Guerra Civil Española (1936-1939)*, 2005.

MOLINA FRANCO, Lucas and MANRIQUE GARCIA, José Mª: *Legión Cóndor. La historia olvidada*, 2000.

MOLINA FRANCO, Lucas and MANRIQUE GARCIA, José Mª: *Los hombres de von Thoma. El Ejército alemán en la Guerra de España (1936/39)*, 2003.

MOMBEEK, Eric *Jagdwaffe: The Spanish civil war*, 1999.

OVEN, Wilfried von: *Hitler y la Guerra Civil española. Misión y destino de la Legión Cóndor*, 1987.

PROCTOR, Raymond L.: *Hitler's Luftwaffe in the Spanish civil war*, 1983.

RIES, Karl and RING, Hans: *The Legion Condor. A History of the Luftwaffe in the Spanish civil war, 1936-1939*, 1992.

STACHE, Rudolf *Armee mit geheimen Auftrag: Die Deutsche Legion Condor in Spanien*, 1939.

TRAUTLOFT, Hannes *Als Jagdflieger in Spanien: Aus dem Tagebuch eines deutschen Legionärs*, 1939.

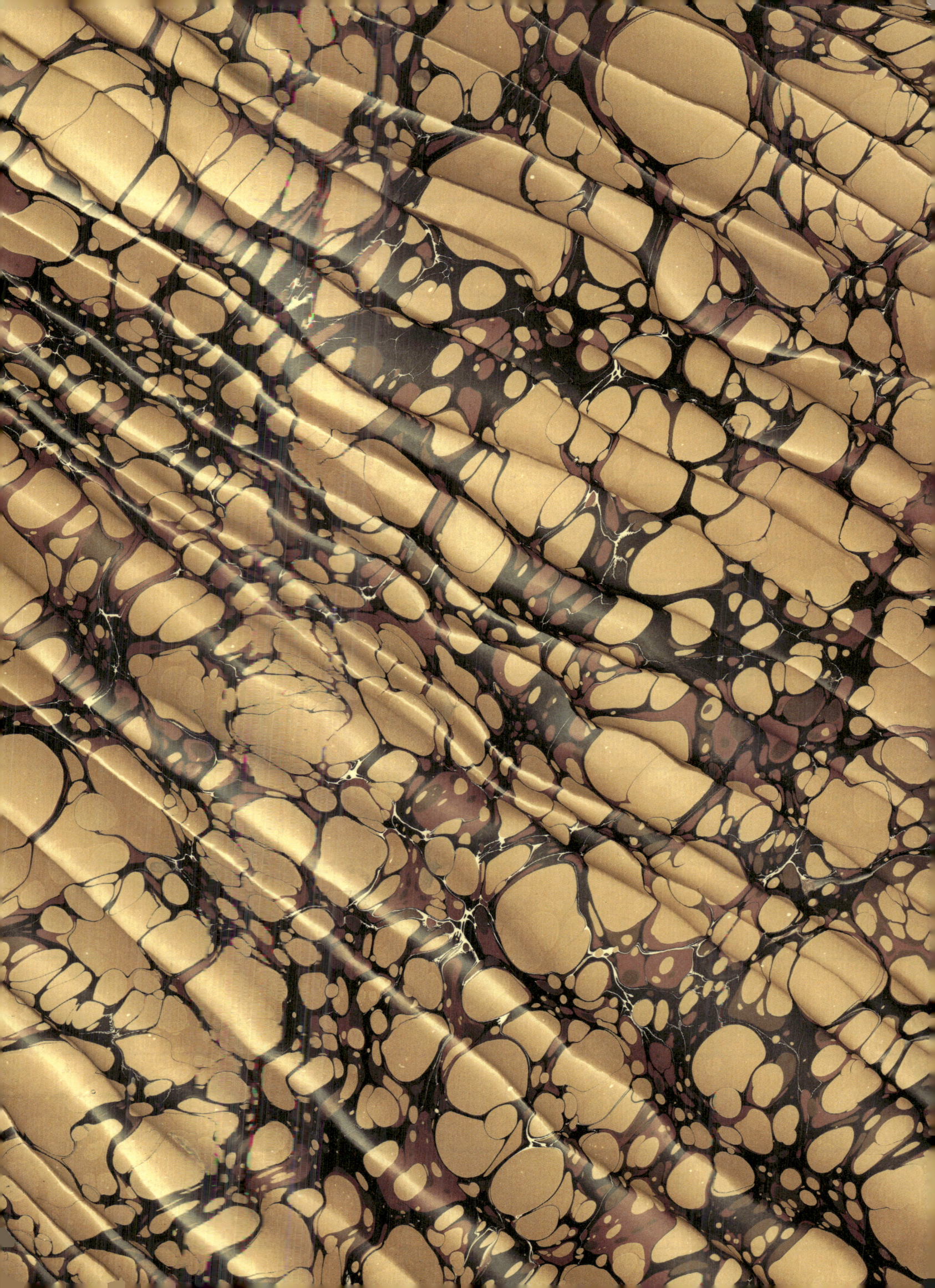